SURVIVING TO THRIVING

A SINGLE PARENT'S PRACTICAL GUIDE TO POST DIVORCE FALLOUT

TORREY COMMISSO

THERAPYWITHTORREY.COM

ISBN· 978-1-7371573-0-4
ISBN: 978-1-7371573-1-1

Front cover image by Samantha Jaquez.
Book design by Steve Commisso.

Printed by KDP Publishing, in the United States of America.

First printing edition 2021.

Publisher Contact info:
TorreytheTherapist@gmail.com
24632 San Juan Avenue, Suite #110
Dana Point, CA 92629

www.TherapywithTorrey.com

TABLE OF CONTENTS

The Road Not Taken
By Robert Frost

Two roads diverged in a yellow wood,
And sorry I could not travel both
And be one traveler, long I stood
And looked down one as far as I could
To where it bent in the undergrowth;

Then took the other, as just as fair,
And having perhaps the better claim,
Because it was grassy and wanted wear;
Though as for that the passing there
Had worn them really about the same,

And both that morning equally lay
In leaves no step had trodden black.
Oh, I kept the first for another day!
Yet knowing how way leads on to way,
I doubted if I should ever come back.

I shall be telling this with a sigh
Somewhere ages and ages hence:
Two roads diverged in a wood, and I —
I took the one less traveled by,
And that has made all the difference.

1

THE ROAD LESS TRAVELED

YOU ARE NOT ALONE. Right now, you might feel more alone than ever before. But unfortunately, at any given moment, there are so many women who are experiencing the soul-twisting pain you are in. I will walk this journey with you, and my heart is to create community to uplift and inspire women just like you to be a better version of themselves as they recover from the wounds of divorce.

Throughout my own journey to move from simply surviving to eventually thriving, my war cry has been, "Don't let all this pain be for nothing." This is how my own divorce story started, it's my why that has pushed me through my darkest days. Desperately longing to find purpose in the pain I was enduring, I decided to dig deep to do the hard work so that I wouldn't continue building unhealthy relationships with a different variation of the same thing again. I wanted

real change; I knew it wouldn't be easy. If that's you —
if you're ready to do the hard work — then read on. If
not, then there are plenty of other books to complain
about how hard going through divorce is and how to
find momentary happiness. Plenty of people choose
that path, but I pray you choose the less traveled and
more difficult path towards thriving.

I am not just an outsider looking in; I am a
Licensed Professional Clinical Counselor in the dual
role as someone who has also walked through the
refining fire of divorce. Not only can I speak from clinical knowledge and research but from my own
scars. Yeah, a scar — that's what divorce leaves you
with. If you're on the front end of divorce, it's probably
more of a gut slice at this point. I promise you it will get
better; one way or another you will heal. Like most
wounds though, you face choices in how to care for the
injury, and part of that comes from assessing your
symptoms.

This book is designed to be a very practical guide.
While of course, as the author, I want you to read every
word of it, I also realize the reality of single parenting;
which isn't the most conducive to free reading time.
That's why I've created this guide to allow you to triage
your "symptoms" by jumping to the most relevant
chapters first. Whether you feel alone and none of your
friends can relate, or you're just trying to figure out
how to tell your kids, I tried to break up the chapters
by subject to allow you to seek answers quickly.

Since I'm also a therapist, this practical guide also deals with emotions because there are so many of them in divorce! When I say we're going to talk about emotions, what I really mean is we're going to figure out what to do with them and how to use them to motivate change. Give yourself grace, there's a chapter on that. We're going to figure out what self-care actually is, not just according to Pinterest.

Throughout this book you will see the phrase "dig deep." The premise is that deep inside of you, you are enough, and you have what it takes. You are alive on this earth for a reason. While that may be an unfathomable concept to take in right now, bear with me, you will survive this. In fact, you just might thrive because of this experience. Right now, I want to leave you with the image from Robert Frost's poem that started this book, "Two roads diverged in a yellow wood." You are in the "yellow wood" and the path of life hit a bump when your marriage ended. Now there's a fork in the path; you get to decide which path you're going to take. You can be the victim of a marriage gone south and your ex-spouse ruining your life, OR you can choose to shake things up and fight the good fight to get your life right. Your choice. I recommend the latter, as the poem says, "and that has made all the difference." I know it has made all the difference for me, and I want that for you.

Lastly, I want to set your expectations on what this guide is not. I won't lie, divorce is hard and

COMPLEX. I'm pretty sure you wouldn't have picked up this book if you thought differently. This guide isn't a guarantee that you're going to live happily ever after. Like so many things, divorce will change you ... some for the better, some for the worse. You get to pick your path. You get to choose if you're willing to do the hard work. Ultimately you choose where this path will take you. Let's transform you into the best version of you. I don't want all your pain to be for nothing.

THE IED EXPLOSION

THERE IS ONE IMPORTANT REALITY that outsiders don't seem to understand about divorce: you were walking along the road and it blew open! Think of it like the military vehicles that are driving along the road in a combat zone focused on their mission. They may know and understand the very real possibility that there may be an IED (Improvised Explosive Device) planted in the road, but the moment it actually explodes, I can't imagine they ever truly expect it. That image definitely resonates with me.

In my own marriage, I knew things were bad. In fact, my ex threw "divorce" on the table all the time for many years, but I had come to acknowledge that this was just our new normal. I found some great resources to help me cope with a destructive marriage and sort of accepted it … until I didn't. I'm actually the one who decided I was no longer willing to tolerate certain behaviors. I thought that when I put my foot down and declared those behaviors unacceptable, he would choose me and our family. Boy, was I wrong.

So here you are in this moment, the moment you realize that this is for real. That this isn't just another separation you can hide from the world, but that it is really 100% over. You were walking on a path with some idea and vision for your future, the IED went off, and now you can see nothing. Everything feels so overwhelming. Maybe you're stumbling around in a state of shock at what has become of your life. Maybe you feel set free. Maybe you feel happier than you've felt in a long time. Maybe you feel guilty. Maybe you feel angry. Maybe you feel all those things and a million more. And that's okay. There's no wrong emotion, but I want you to learn the importance of what you do with your emotions.

I remember my dad telling me a quote from Winston Churchill, "If you're going through hell, keep going." There's great truth to that. The moral is: Don't get stuck in the yucky, frontend emotions of divorce. You might have every reason to be bitter, but *justice is not your job*. Let me repeat that, justice is not your job. It's not the judge's job either. What, wait!? Everything in me hates that! I so badly want life to be fair. Like not exactly fair, but mostly fair, or at least sort of fair. Can you relate to that? It's so hard to look at all the tragedies of the world and come to terms with the fact that life is just not fair. Divorce is no different. It's just not fair.

As a therapist, I can predict that there is a correlation between your need for things to be fair and how much anger you are experiencing in the divorce process. Here's where you can dig in: What are you going to do about your anger? The emotion is no doubt justified; I'm not asking you to tamp that down. Let me tell you, that does not work.

Think of anger like an energy source. Like a dog that hasn't been walked, you must get rid of the energy or it will wreak havoc in your home. My biggest piece of advice: Move your body — a lot. Sweat ... it's like a different version of crying. *Think of it like crying through your armpits.* Sometimes both happen, whatever. Let me be clear, I'm not saying to go take a nice walk around the block. Freaking climb a mountain. Finally do the Beachbody P90X workout series. Consider a new sport or activity. Maybe join that community soccer team. But do something that's so hard that you're not sure that you can complete it.

For some of us Type A people, it's a great time to sign up for a half marathon or a triathlon. When so many things in our life are out of our control, sometimes it's helpful to have something like a training schedule to focus on and accomplish. For others, it's not the time. You may not know what your custody schedule is going to look like, or maybe you have all the custody and a childcare nightmare on your hands.

Don't lose sight of the goal, sweat your anger out. Figure out a way. There are plenty of workouts online or on Instagram or Facebook groups - for free! Don't make excuses.

You can do this; you need to do this! For you. Yep, for you. But also for your kids and just about everyone else in your life that will benefit from you sweating out your anger instead of letting it subconsciously spill on those around you. Consider it time well spent. You've got to get you right. You are strong and you have what it takes. Let's take a moment to confirm that. Below I want you to list out five hard things that you've done or overcome. I don't care if you have to think back to elementary school, I know they are there. If you can't think of them, note that your thinking might be askew in the messages you tell yourself. Flag that to discuss with your therapist. More on therapy later in Chapter 10. Now give it a try.

5 Hard Things I've Accomplished or Overcome:

1. _____
2. _____
3. _____
4. _____
5. _____

Okay, so how hard was that? Be honest with yourself. Why is this activity so important? When we get through hard things it builds our confidence to get through more hard things. Here's what I know: everyone goes through hard things. Sometimes it takes a good friend or therapist to legitimize that they were hard. Wait, what? I'm serious, "hard" is a relative term. And what's hard for one person may not be so hard for someone else. Nobody gets to tell you that your thing wasn't hard though. If it was hard for you, that's what I want listed above.

Let me give you an example to help clarify what I mean. I had the bright idea to go back to get my master's degree in my late 20's. I decided to quit my job in order to do this. I also had a one-year-old at home and got pregnant in my second year of the program. To some of you, this may sound overwhelmingly hard and unimaginable to complete. Others might think, oh how lovely, you didn't have to work while trying to complete the program. In hindsight, I view it as a lot of logistics and planning that needed to happen. I had many melt-downs and considered quitting many times because it often felt like too much. The point being: "hard" is relative, it's based on our prior experiences. Not your best friend's prior experiences, not your sister's prior experiences, not your boss' prior experiences … yours.

Take a moment again. Close your eyes, breathe in as much air as you can through your nose and slowly push all of the air out of your lungs, through your mouth. Do this five times. Think about the times you cried, really hard, like ugly cried. What have you failed

9

at? Who has died close to you? What job did you have to work really hard to get or keep or get fired from? What happened next? Think in that space. How did you handle it? What did you learn? How did it change you? I swear those things are there, so dig deep.

Let's go back to the image I painted at the beginning of this chapter: the IED explosion. Your world has just been shattered. You are in it right now. But let's talk about being a survivor for a second. Surviving doesn't mean pretending like it did not or is not happening. Surviving means you got through it. While it kills some, it is not going to kill you. You will get through this.

It is hard to drive real motivation without being mistaken for cheesy. I will try to authentically be your cheerleader, not because your tears make me uncomfortable but because I want more for you. Now is the time for a mantra. Whether you're spiritual or not, you need a mantra — one that works for you. This is an ever-changing area for me depending on where my current struggle is. I can give you some suggestions, but only you can figure out the one you need. Yep, you NEED one. In a time when you are fighting so much negative energy, you need positive power. For some, this can be a Bible verse. I think Bible verses carry a tremendous amount of power. (Disclaimer: While my faith is central to my story, I want to write this book in a way that's universal and can reach you, whatever you believe. It may be a time to reconnect with the faith of your childhood or to try something new.) So here are some universal mantras:

- I can't choose my emotions, but I can choose my path.
- I will honor my higher power (God?) in all I do.
- I will survive.
- May my heart be kind, my mind fierce, and my spirit brave.
- Create a life you can be proud of.
- Be a warrior not a worrier.
- Don't let yesterday take up too much of today.
- I am enough.
- Every day is a new day.
- Choose purpose over perfect.
- I am resilient.
- Be strong enough to stand alone.
- Find a way or make one.

For more ideas check out my website: *Surviving2Thriving.life*. For now, just pick one. Try it out; if it's not affirming then try another one until you find one that works for you. Pinterest has many more ideas. Think on this, meditate on this, breathe this, write it on your mirror, make it your phone screen. You're going to need this to get through the coming days. But here's the key thing: you will get through the coming days.

Sometimes people are in our life to show us what to do. I want you to flip it for a second: envision the person you do not want to become. What does she look like? How does she spend her time? How does she feel about life in general? How are the other relationships in her life doing? Use that to motivate you away from becoming that person. Remember, divorce will change you, but that doesn't mean it's for the better. Sometimes you have to be in touch with what you don't want.

In Rachel Hollis' book, *I Didn't See That Coming*, she writes, "Don't fear your own weakness, fear drowning in despair for the rest of your time on earth because you were too afraid to confront your pain." Now is the time to confront your pain. You survived the most devastating emotional IED in your life and now choosing to move forward, while confronting your anger and your pain along the way, takes so much courage. But trust me, it is so worth it and makes all the difference for the rest of your life.

3

CO-PARENTING 101
STARTS WITH TELLING THE KIDS

SO YOU REALIZED YOUR MARRIAGE IS OVER, now what? Oh man, now you have to tell those precious little (or not so little) people the bad news. Bummer! How the heck do you do that? How much do you tell them? Believe it or not, I think this initial conversation really sets the tone for what's to come in the days ahead both in the kids' interpretation and in what kind of co-parents you're going to be. If you're already past this conversation and you totally blew it, that's fine. Perfection is not the expectation. There is what's ideal ... than there's reality. I am very aware of the valley between the two, that's where I live. The good news is that kids are extremely forgiving if you just ask. They're also extremely resilient. They want world peace, at least peace in their own world as they know it (a.k.a. their home).

Let's begin with the concept of co-parents. I've

actually come to like this once-foreign term. It's the idea that while you're no longer husband and wife, there is still a teamwork mentality. The goal is that you participate in parenting together even though the marriage has ended. Now, I know the vision of team-work isn't always reality. Seriously, trust me! My own story started off looking more like two toddlers fighting over the last cookie but with time it has gotten way better. This may or may not be your story but I'm going to speak to the majority here and we'll call it your new ideal or vision for the future.

Starting with what co-parenting is not: co-parenting doesn't mean buddies. You are aiming for a civil relationship. There's a great checklist of successful co-parenting benchmarks in Chapter 11, but let's focus on how to set the tone for now. I know that there are those rare, divorced couples who end up being besties (if I'm honest, I don't really understand that and I'm going to try really hard not to judge things that I don't understand). What I do understand though, is strug-gling not to hate your ex, and I'm going to confidently assume that this is the vast majority of us. *Hate is a choice.* I know that's a crappy thing to tell you right now in the thick of it — sorry, not sorry. Be pissed, but remember the last chapter? Set the book down and go exercise if you need to, but come back. Part of what makes me a good counselor is that I say the hard things. I speak truth even when it totally sucks.

Yay, you're still reading! Okay, so I get the hate

struggle. Hate oozes like a nasty infection — we'll call it an infection of the heart. I like what Rick Warren said (roughly quoted), "Hate is like drinking poison hoping that the other person will die." If your hate is not dealt with, it will kill you, metaphorically speaking. Although, there is some research that points to the increased likelihood of some serious medical issues when you harbor hate. You're going to have to fight this battle for your own sake. I'm not even talking "so you can one day go to heaven." I'm talking about "you're all you can be while here on Earth." Then you can be the person you were designed to be. You can't be that person if your heart is festering hate.

Hate is the result of resentment and anger. In the last chapter we talked about what to do with anger, but let's take a moment to talk about resentment. Resentment is a conscious choice. Yes, it can be the result of all the negative actions someone else did to us, but it's ultimately your choice. Oh, I'm sorry, more truth that is hard to hear? You have a choice. So, make it a positive choice that is in line with the person you want to be. Sounds simple enough, but it's hard — really, really hard. In fact, it's much easier to justify your hate, as many people do. That does not mean it's in your best interest though. Eventually, to get to thriving, you're going to have to begin the process towards forgiveness. I try to be a reasonable person, so I definitely recognize that's likely not feasible in the early stages of divorce. We will tackle that mountain in Chapter 15 near the end of this book. Spoiler alert: you will get stuck being a growly, bitter woman if you don't work that process. We can table that for now though and focus on the tornado of decisions swirling around you.

Let's circle back to that poem by Robert Frost that starts out this book. This is that moment where "two roads diverged in a yellow wood." You are at the fork. Which path will you choose? It's going to make all the difference in not only the coming days but the coming years!

I never tell my clients to *not* think about something. That never works. As you work towards mental wellness, embrace the concept of *thought replacement*. Let me elaborate: envision your child scared after a nightmare. If you tell them, "just don't think about it," that totally doesn't work. It's all they can think about! You must replace the thoughts and tell them to think about other things that are not scary so they can relax and go back to sleep.

Let's apply this to where you might be at now. Telling you *not* to think about all the stupid things your ex did (or is currently doing) is not helpful. Here's the active choice you need to make to put you on that road less traveled. Choose to think about the things that lift you up. You are at a stage that is so easy to get bogged down and overwhelmed. Take some deep breaths. Side note, it's very common in the early days to struggle with the urge to have a panic attack. Your mantra and slow deep breathing will be key elements from this survival first-aid kit. Believe that you have what it takes to get through today — just today. You will figure this out.

In your calm state, think of what you need to do today. I'm not talking about what you *want* to get done, but what do you *need* to get done today. Write it down, make a list with nice little checkboxes, or put it in your phone. Here's the reality of stress: you forget stuff. Also, when you complete that nice little list of the things you needed to get done, it will build your confidence that you survived a hard day and that will make you feel a better about your likelihood of surviving the next day.

That said, I realize that not everyone's early days are that hard to survive. You might be very happy to have physical distance from your ex. Also, it is possible to feel both. You might be in a stage of shock early on in your divorce. Sometimes, especially if divorce is thrown on the table because of an affair, you may just be in a state of disbelief. That's okay — just keep walking and don't forget to eat something a few times a day, even if you're not hungry.

You might be thinking: "I thought this chapter was on co-parenting?" It is. First you have to be able to come to the table with your co-parent without socking them in the face. I'm serious! Just me? While it might feel great in the moment, it's not good for the kids and probably won't look good if it comes up in the court-room. If you haven't told the kids yet, it's time to rip the bandage off. If at all possible, try to have a pre-meeting with the other parent to discuss how you are going to present the information and why that specific plan is best (you need their buy-in not just compliance).

What the heck do you say? Give yourself grace. You have likely never done this before. I can't give you a script, okay I could, but kids are intuitive, and they'll know if you're not being authentic. Darn! What you say largely depends on the age(s) of your children. Here's a little breakdown:

0-1 year old: You don't need to tell them. Watch your tone whether you're talking to your ex-spouse or a friend on the phone. Babies are intuitive. They will feel unsafe if you are a hot mess of emotions. Figuring out how to cope with your emotions in a healthy way will help them feel safe. Make sure both parents are seeing the baby regularly, even if it's just a few hours a couple times a week. *Consistency is critical for infants.*

1-4 years old: Keep it super simple. You don't need to use the word "divorce" or try to explain it. Just *focus on logistics.* The conversation is super short and simple; think facts. For example: "Daddy and I are getting unmarried. That means our family is going to change. We are going to live in different houses, but you get to live at both. We are going to try really hard to share you now and you can always call the parent you're not with if you miss them." Not in the initial conversation but maybe in the coming couple weeks, there's a great book to read with them called "Dinosaurs Do Divorce" that explains logistics in more detail. A daily call time can also be helpful at this age but beware of not having it too close to bedtime, as it could make them sad and interfere with sleep. Kids just don't handle the hard stuff as well when they are tired. Consider each parent giving the child a stuffed animal to take to the other parent's house to snuggle and love on when that parent is not physically with them. Crying is okay and healthy. It's a natural emotion and often cuddles help. Having consistent rules, bedtime, bedtime routines and even food between households will help their sense of stability.

5-11 years old: Consistency is critical to their sense of security. They may struggle with feeling like one parent is at fault and/or that one of the parents is divorcing them. It is essential to emphasize and re-emphasize that the decision had absolutely nothing to do with their behavior or what color socks they wore that morning. You may see regression of thumb-sucking or attention-seeking behavior as they experiment in this new concept of family life. Encourage them to view it just as a change, and that's how you want to word it when telling them that you are getting divorced. You can relate it to changing schools. If that is a change that they have previously experienced, you can build on that. Point out the things they liked with that change and what they did well when they changed schools, even if it was just changing from preschool to elementary school.

This age will have lots of logistical questions, especially the younger grades. I encourage you to *only answer the questions they are asking — with facts*. You don't need to explain the "why" behind that information as it will likely be overwhelming and simply not helpful — it can even be hurtful. A consistent regular schedule can help ease the stress at this age a lot. Additionally, having or more specifically not having "their stuff" at the right house can be stressful. There's a lot to that topic and I'll cover it more in the next chapter. For now, it is just something to be mindful of as a potential trigger for them. Watch for somatic symptoms. That's a fancy word for the headaches or stomach aches that are a physiological response to the stress of the divorce, often on days they transition between households. This is a very real thing and will be discussed more in the next chapter.

Middle School aged: So, as if having a middle schooler wasn't hard enough, bless you if you happen to have a middle schooler during this rough chapter of life. Here's the most important thing: *keep them out of the conflict, decisions and conversations.* Anytime you can make a decision for them, do! As is common with many topics at this age, they may seem like they have the maturity and are tracking right along with what you are saying, and they very well may be… but emotionally, it's too much! Do you remember middle school? You may have cried more at that time than you do in your divorce process; the only difference is now you know what you're crying about. With boys, you may see an increase in anger. Now, let me be clear, I'm not saying to make it an off-limits topic, I am saying to view your job as a listener, asking open-ended questions, and to let them do all the talking. More in the next chapter on the importance and skill of asking open-ended questions. This age will be heavily into trying to answer the "why" questions around the divorce, but you must build your fence and protect this information. *Turn their questions back to them.* "Why is it important for you to know?" Ideally, and trust me, I know this is a big "ideally," if you and your ex-spouse can be on the same page here that will make a world of difference in what we'll call *divorce damage control*. Begin to use the phrase if you don't already, "it's not in your best interest to know." If you can encourage them to talk to some of the other adults in their life, this is often helpful.

High School aged: This actually might be the most challenging age. Unlike any of the other age groups, your teenager has likely individualized to some extent, and you are less likely to walk in this emotional journey with them or even know much about their process. Know that it's definitely brewing though. *A support system is essential for this age*, and unlike most of the other ages, it is unlikely that the core of their support system is Mom or Dad.
There are two big misconceptions parents tend to bump into. One, they think that because their child is still getting good grades and not acting out that they are coping just fine. While this may be true, don't stop there. For this age, it's really important to keep checking in. They are much more likely to mimic a grief process and will experience stages of loss. What that means is that while they may not be mad at you one day, they may be very sad or angry the next day.

Encourage them that all the emotions are okay, and you are feeling a lot that changes day to day, too. You can adult with them a tiny bit here, but keep the focus on them and don't share your specifics. Oftentimes, this age feels the pressure of keeping it together because their parents are falling apart. You want them to be able to fall apart, too. Again, like with a middle schooler, *utilize a lot of open-ended questions and active listening.* Really encourage them to talk about it with someone but assure them it doesn't have to be with you; someone one older that they respect can be a great alternative. I don't recommend that they dive deep into social media relationships with people they don't know that are also going through divorce. Trust me, I have worked with a lot of teens and this is likely their natural course. You will want to have an open conversation about how it's not in their best interest. The second frequent misconception is: thinking that they don't need to talk about it. They do, it's a big deal.

My last recommendation for this age is to have consistent rules between households, if possible, as this will decrease the likelihood of your teen acting out or testing what they can get away with. Set not only clear expectations on home-work/grades, curfew times, cell phone rules, social media, and driving, but also what the consequences of violating those rules will be. Getting on the same page proactively with the other parent will help alleviate some of the stress and emotion for everyone when there is a violation. Consider creating a contract type document for the parents and teen to sign. Hey, maybe you'll end up being better parents post-divorce than when you were married! Dare to dream!

Consider having one main talk with all the children then telling them you'd like to meet with them individually to answer their questions or any concerns that they might have. What you don't want is for one child to raise concerns that aren't even on a younger child's radar. Think of it like running damage control.

I'll be honest, this will be a gruelingly and heart-breaking time. It is absolutely the time to stuff your emotions down and be the strong one. You want to present the overall message: "Everything is going to be okay — our family is just going to look different now." Establishing a sense of security is critical for them at this step. When parents can both present this information in a calm manner, it sets the tone.

If you are highly emotional, consider keeping your message short and let them know you will talk to them more later that day or week, but right now it's too hard for you to talk about. This is the beginning of showing them that you are going to handle your emotions separate from theirs. If you have a teen or even just a sweet child that is a good listener, it can be tempting to use them to emotionally process yourself. This is a tremendous burden for them to carry and will have lasting effects on them whether it is trouble sleeping, general anxiety or loss of joy.

Your job is to model healthy coping. It will help you and it will help them. Example: With younger children, coloring can be very soothing. I think it's a great activity when I'm too exhausted emotionally or physically. Sometimes they'll talk, or sometimes we just color. It's very relaxing and lets your mind wander. Even tweens who haven't colored in a while might start enjoying this activity again. Hint: a new set of colored pencils can help jumpstart their willingness. Other activities you might consider modeling to encourage healthy coping include:

- Taking a walk
- Doing a meditation
- Stretch your body
- Read a "for fun" book
- Take a dance party break
- Take a shower
- Do a puzzle
- Drink something warm like tea slowly enjoying each sip

I will wrap up our co-parenting 101 by emphasizing

the critical concept that my counselor beat me over the head with: "*stop answering questions they're not asking.*" This was a profound concept to me. As I searched for answers in my floundering early days of divorce, I'll be honest, my best mommy heart dumbly thought that surely my kids had a ton of questions, too! It turns out, they really didn't. I was shocked. When I stopped trying to explain everything and every change to them and just gave them facts followed by, "Does that make sense? Do you have any questions about that?" I couldn't believe how often they responded with "nope" or their questions were more on the simple logistics. Prime example, I was freaking out on what to tell my kids or how to explain to them the concept of a super-vised visit. As a therapist, I naturally turned to the team of therapists I worked with and no one really had a good solid answer that I liked. I asked the supervisor, and she advised, "Oh, just tell them they get to see their dad this afternoon and Jolene will be there. They prob-ably won't even ask who Jolene is." I totally doubted her, but since I was at a sheer loss and she seemed pretty confident, I decided to give it a try. Sure enough, she was right! And when I tacked on my simple open-ended questions "Does that make sense? Do you have any questions about that?" Guess what: the only ques-tion I got was, "Can I bring my doll?"

Older kids can be trickier in this area because they may have more questions, but they may not be asking them. That's actually okay. It's a great time to encourage them to see a counselor, a mentor, or youth group leader. Often a neutral party for them to process with is much healthier. Give them that gift. Let them know that their friends may not be talking to them about it because they don't know what to say or assume that they don't want to talk about it. Encourage them it's okay to bring it up with friends and that they blanket the conversation by utilizing the phrase, "It's okay if you don't know what to say, I just wanted to talk about it a little with someone close to me." It's a good life skill. Believe it or not, there can be good things that come out of divorce for your kids. I mean, just the active teaching of healthy coping skills that might have not otherwise happen, is huge.

Don't go patting yourself on the back too much for giving your kids "the gift" of divorce though. Just like it's tough for you, it's obviously very tough for them. There are so many emotions and some grace is definitely going to be needed for all those around. I would encourage you to notify their teacher(s) and school counselor (their e-mail address is likely on the school's website). Just putting it on everyone's radar can be helpful and can put a lens on what they might be observing in the classroom. It also adds another support person to your child's safety net.

You don't need to tell the teachers any of the "why you're getting divorced" story, just that you are. If you know what your custody schedule is going to be, that information might be helpful to them, too. Also open the door for future conversations with, "If you notice any new or unusual behavior about my child, I would appreciate knowing that, too." It's not unusual for teens to test newly single and often busy parents to see what they can get away with not doing, often as a way of testing if you still care about them. It even happens on a subconscious level sometimes.

I know that was a lot to take in. I'll also be real in that much of this I learned the hard way or heard in other people's stories. Don't expect yourself to do it perfectly. I encourage you to just put effort in parenting with intentionality. Move the marker away from "doing it right" to just keeping your eye on the path you are trying to clumsy walk along as best you can. Give yourself grace when you fall to get back up, dust yourself off and keep walking! As much as humanly possible, try to maintain being the consistent parent to them that you always have, whatever that is.

4

CO-PARENTING

LOGISTICS

YOU TOLD THE KIDS. One parent has probably moved out, but still you have a ton of questions over the logistics. If you're like me, in those early stages of divorce, you don't really know anyone in your same season of life. Before I walked this path myself, I was such a judgmental jerk. If I'm being honest, I didn't respect other women who were divorced. But then, if I take a step back and give myself a little bit of grace, I can say it was because I knew how extremely hard I was fighting and what it was taking me to stay in a bad marriage. I thought that if I could suffer through my marriage, surely, they could, too! How dare they get divorced? Ultimately, I was humbled. Thanks, God! Now I live in a place of no judgement: not only about divorce but most anything. I discovered a really important truth in all of this: I don't know their story and it's

not my place to judge — their life, their choice, their
actions … their path.

That said, let's talk about some of the nitty gritty
logistics that brings us to the second stage of co-parenting. We can start with the fun subject of what goes
between households. My obnoxious over-simplified
answer: Whatever you want! What I mean is, I think
it's ideal to let the kids figure this one out if possible,
with a few ground rules of course.

If you can, let them drag as much stuff as they want
back and forth in the beginning stages; this eases the
transition for them early on and they usually get tired
of it. Eventually they figure out what they want at each
house. One thing with younger kids that I found
worked well was trying to divide toys into categories.
For example, have all the Legos at one parent's house
and have all the doll stuff at the other parent's house.
This worked on a lot of levels and also made gift-giving
a little easier. Having different toy categories at each
home helps the child to look forward to playing with
their different toys at the other house, rather than just
providing two sets of everything. It also helps curate
the idea of different households being okay. I do think
having games and craft supplies at both households is
important though.

Technology

Setting ground rules together on "stuff" can be tricky. Ideally, try to have separate technology (computers/tablets) at each household. If you do allow them to go between households, agree in advance (in writing!) if the item is lost, stolen or broken, who will pay for the replacement. Sounds silly, but if you know this in advance, it will actually benefit your child from being placed in the middle. Phones inevitably go back and forth, but I also encourage you to have a proactive agreement with the other parent regarding who pays for the replacement item if it is lost, stolen or broken here, too. Often, parents vary in their views on what's okay for tech usage. If you want to make a change only relevant for your household (because you can't dictate what the other parent does at their house), now is a great time to parent the way you feel is best. Perk of divorce: you don't have to agree on best parenting practices anymore! Although it is still ideal to be consistent for your child's sake.

Clothing

What about clothes? The short answer, each household should have enough for the child during their parenting time. This is so much easier said than done. Wait, so I send them to school in "Mom Clothes" on Friday but when he brings them back to Mom's house on Sunday night they're wearing "Dad Clothes"? Okay, here's the ideal in this scenario: Dad has a small bin near the children's room that he has them trained to throw their "Mom Clothes" or anything they want to return to Mom's house, and Dad bags the clothes/items on Sunday before dropping those and the kids back to Mom on Sunday evening. Mom has a similar bin at her house outside their rooms where kids are trained to drop their "Dad Clothes" they wore home to Mom's house on Sunday evening. Mom then returns the dad clothes to Dad next time there is interaction. And the cycle lives on and on. That's ideal. The reality is, if your kids are anything like mine, they struggle to remember consistently. Think about this for a backup plan: each parent has a symbol they draw on the tag when they purchase kid clothes. For example, heart for Mom, star for Dad. Then when clean laundry is being folded, the folder (no judgement if your perfect little angel doesn't do their own laundry) looks for the symbols and tosses any of the other parents' clothing in the bin to return on the next kid swap.

I think shoes are inevitably shared and it's sort of wasteful to have two totally separate sets, but that's just my opinion. It also depends on whether the other parent is good at bringing the requested type of shoes when, for example, dress shoes are needed for an upcoming visit. Overall, I just encourage open communication between parents on this subject. Key phrase being, *between parents,* as the kids can feel very in the middle and stress on this subject. I also encourage you to be as generous as possible in your assumptions toward the other parent. It will benefit you to not come at them assuming the worst case or that they're intentionally being a jerk. You know how you're extra stressed and tired lately? So are they. Give them the grace that you hope they give you.

One last point on the clothes topic before we move on. One little detail that I realized early on: if possible, be the one to carry the clothes bag to hand to the other parent or place at their door. Think of it as a little burden you can ease for your child. It is emotionally difficult for children to move between homes. Carrying stuff — honestly anything — makes it harder. Think of it like the kid who hates school. Loading their backpack up with a bunch of heavy books and binders makes walking into school that much more undesirable.

Gifts

Let's talk about gifts. As life goes on and birthdays and holidays approach, this area inevitably needs to be thought about and discussed in advance with the other parent (ideally). Most divorced parents that I know try to implement the general rule that the gift stays at the parent's house who gave it. For example, Mom gives child an American Girl doll so the American Girl doll stays at Mom's house. This extends to the family members related to Mom, too.

Notice I say general rule because I think making exceptions right after the gift is given *can* be okay. Building on the example above, say your child is extremely excited about the American Girl doll she just got and Dad is picking her up tomorrow morning for the weekend, consider letting her take it to Dad's house as a special exception. Let her know ahead of time it's a special exception though and clarify that this is not the new normal.

Other parents are very loose in this area. I think part of the equation is how easy is it for the child to move items between households and noting if there is a tendency for stuff to migrate mostly to one house without coming back. This is a great area to generously give the other parent the benefit of the doubt that they are simply not aware of the disparity between households. In discussing, perhaps cite some examples to make your point, and be future focused with some suggestions of how to correct the issue. For example, implementing a "Mom Bin" while at Dad's house or a box by the front door.

Birthday Parties

We can't talk about gifts without talking about birthday parties. I haven't seen a consensus here, so I'll just give you some ideas of what I've seen work. For some families, one parent loves the planning and hosting of parties and this has been their domain. Consider letting that parent keep this established area. It may be one way that parent likes to show love for their child and will really feel like a hole if they have to share it. Or maybe, one parent is happy to relinquish the burden of party hosting, so long as the other parent is allowed to attend. Or, if your kid hits the jackpot, maybe both parents throw the child separate parties since they may have different friends at each household and/or different extended family that they want to celebrate with. Just don't turn it into a competition; no one wins. The parent that doesn't usually throw parties may do it quite differently than the child is used to. This is okay in the years to come, but at least in the first few years, let it feel as normal as possible to the child. Remember, *the goal is stability and consistency to create a new sense of security.*

In the case that the parents equally shared the task of birthday parties, consider alternating years. This one is pretty logical, so I won't elaborate other than encouraging the parent to get creative in their definition of "party." Because divorce is expensive and the household budget has potentially been split in half, I want to encourage you that parties don't have to be expensive to be wonderful from a child's perspective. You may feel that you no longer have a home that is conducive to a large number of people, but don't let that be a barrier! Just get creative.

One of the easiest ways to cut costs on parties, that has very little impact on the overall event, is to not serve a meal. Choose a time that is obviously between meals. After school or late morning can be a great time for toddlers. Consider selling your teen on a few friends coming over for a sleepover instead of twenty teenagers that eat a ton in the evening hours.

Another way to increase the fun factor is to add a theme. All ages enjoy this! It could be an 80s sleepover for your teen where they dress like the 80s, watch *The Breakfast Club*, snack on things filled with red dye and drink Tang. Or for your younger child, have a kitty theme where they dress like kitties (you can usually find cheap party packs of kitty ears on Amazon). You can have a fishy-cracker eating contest from bowls on the floor, play kitty trivia to test their cat knowledge, and even meow out happy birthday rather than sing the song. Kids love to play Freeze Dance or bring back Charades to match your party theme. Even just asking everyone to wear as much of the birthday boy or girl's favorite color can be fun. Try and find food that is that color and use dollar store decorations. Pinterest is great for cheap birthday ideas.

I can throw out all these great ideas, but I also want to keep it real. Generally, I absolutely love to plan parties for the upcoming birthday child and have fun creating our own games, but when less than a month after my separation was one of my daughter's birthday, I was completely overwhelmed amongst many emotions. I gave her the option to have $100 instead of a party. Judge away, but we were both happy with this temporary solution and I was so grateful that she opted-in.

I also recognize that some families don't do birthday parties or do them sporadically. If you do them sporadically, it's probably a good year to skip. If you never do them, stay on that track because you want things to feel as normal as possible to your child. Don't be tempted to outshine your ex-spouse; be mature. If you didn't throw a party because the other parent was against it for whatever reason, consider waiting a year while your child stabilizes. Maybe they've been begging you to throw them a party for the first time, and if you feel up to it, that's okay, too. Clearly there's no one right way to do this. You just have to figure out what makes sense for your family and it may be a bit of a process.

Traditions

It is a great time to make new traditions though! This is a fun topic to converse with your child about so you get their buy-in. In this conversation, share with your child that one of the good things about divorce is that your family gets to hit the reset button and evaluate what they like and don't like about holidays. They may have good ideas they've heard from their friends, and this can be a great conversation to learn more about their circle of influence. By picking their brain, thinking and talking about something other than all the things that they don't like about divorce, they can focus on some positives. Here are a few ideas that I introduced with my kids:

Hair-tober = For the whole month of October, you get to have the hair color of your choice! My kids love this. Prior to divorce, one of my girls really wanted to dye her hair but it didn't really align with the values I was trying to instill. Doing it this way shifted the "why" of hair-dying into a bonding experience.

Chain-of-Fun = On New Year's Eve, I make a paper chain (strips of paper stapled together) and each strip has an activity on it. For example, Name That Tune (create a playlist of songs your family liked from the last year), run a lap around the house, take a shower (sneaky Mommy!), eat a cookie, tell the person to your right something you like about them, share your favorite memory from the last year, share one thing that you want to get better at in the coming year, take a pretend nap for one minute, tell a joke … you get the picture. Then a few hours before you want to call it a night, let them break one chain at a time and do the activity on it.

A silly made up *Scavenger Hunt on Valentine's Day* where the first clue can only be found by popping a whole bunch of balloons. Heart pizza is a must for dinner!

Wear your pajamas all day on Christmas — preferably a onesie — even if you go over to other people's houses.

My mom doesn't love this one when we're having big family gatherings, but my kids love it!

Depending on your custody schedule, it is likely that you don't have them every year for the same holidays. Explain that you can celebrate a little early and make it work for your family. The goal is to build a new family vision that's positive and fun. Once your child realizes holidays might be twice as fun, especially that they just might be getting twice as many gifts, they might feel a tiny bit better about the situation. Well, at least for that day.

Don't beat yourself up that things aren't the way they once were. Give yourself grace. Feel the feelings that surround all the change, whether you journal it out, have a good cry, run, or simply enjoy a slow cup of tea. Most likely, your kids are having mixed feelings too; it's a big change! Invite them to talk about it, where they do most of the talking, and *after* you've tried to tackle your own feelings (bringing them into your awareness). Acknowledge that you are sad and that's okay. This is a big change. Remember the IED explosion? After surviving, now you're beginning to rebuild or at least thinking about what you want to build.

I don't know about you, but I got a little hung up on the word "family." It just didn't feel quite right to refer to my children and myself as a family anymore. Any picture of just my children and I felt incomplete. In the chapter titled "Unsharing" we'll talk about photographs, or more specifically what to do with the old ones.

Let's focus on the importance and fine art of asking your kids unbiased, open-ended questions, especially when it comes to the logistics of co-parenting. An open-ended question is simply a question that cannot be answered with a simple one-word answer like "yes" or "no." It may be your default to ask, "How was your day at school?" when your child gets home. Instead consider rephrasing your question to, "What was the best and worst part of your day?" Likely even the least talkative kids will give you much more information simply because they can't answer that question briefly.

Now believe it or not, you may be asking your kids biased questions without even realizing it when it comes to the other parent and things surrounding that household. In research, we call this survey bias. Survey bias is when a researcher is asking questions a certain way, intentionally or sometimes unintentionally, to support their theory. So crazy that we can actually do this with our kids, too!

Let me give an example. If you are a parent with survey bias you might ask, "Hey Suzy, did Dad have his friends over that drink a lot this weekend?" There are a few things wrong with this question. Let's start with how you might ask this question in an unbiased manner. Instead try, "What did you do this weekend?"

which might lead to their response. "We had a few families over Saturday" and you can ask, "Oh, what'd you do?" and they might say something like, "The parents hung out in the backyard while the kids swam."

Honestly, I don't love that whole line of questioning because it feels a little too much like prying, but I also know that sometimes there are safety concerns. In the scenario above, if they don't tell you that Dad was drinking, you really shouldn't ask as it puts them in the middle. Also, as a counselor, I can say kids generally mention or talk about things they are concerned about. If they don't mention it, they likely weren't concerned. You learned that adults stayed outside while the kids were swimming. Bonus!

Try to ask broad questions. If they tell you something you might think was scary ask, "How did that make you feel?" Rather than asking, "Did you feel scared?" This also opens the door for processing their feelings with them and brainstorming how they might handle the situation differently next time. Always assume the best of the other parent and take whatever your kid is saying with a grain of salt. They don't always get all the details right, at least not 100% of the time. With younger kids below nine years old, know that if they're giving a lot of detail they're probably not lying. If a child nine years old and above gives a lot of detail, it can actually be a sign they're fabricating a story to benefit them.

Let your goal in question-asking be supporting

your child, not information gathering on the other parent. You want your questions to reflect that you care and that you want to listen and support them in all areas of life. Here are some of my favorite open-ended questions (printable cards on my website Surviving2Thriving.life):

- What is one thing you're grateful for today?
- Who did you eat lunch with?
- Tell me about something that made you happy today.
- What makes a good friend?
- Ask about their best friend and how things are going with them.
- Ask them the "why" questions like, "Why do you think there are emotions?"
- What is the main emotion you've been feeling today?
- What's one nice thing you did today?
- What makes a good meal?
- What are you most proud of?
- What do you like about yourself?
- What did you do well today?
- Did you make any good choices that were really hard today?
- What's one thing you will do different tomorrow?
- What magic power do you wish you had?

- Describe what makes a home feel good to you.
- What do you worry about the most?
- If you could fly anywhere, where would it be?
- If you had a magic wand, what would you use it to do?

I also like to engage in "would you rather" questions as a fun way to connect and pass the time when we're driving to their dad's house (an hour away). Sometimes the questions are silly and take a turn south towards toilet talk, "Would you rather pee in your pants or barf on the floor during class?" This turns into a full discussion on the pros and cons of each scenario. The point is just to engage with them on their level and sometimes get them thinking. For example, "Would you rather have your own airplane or save one hundred kittens?" We've had some great discussions with even the silliest of questions.

I've come to cherish this sweet time with them. While they love their devices, I often remind them that devices are a privilege, and they can only have them if they talk to me a bit first. In my case, I divide the talking portion of our drive to the halfway point where we happen to get off a toll road. While one of my children may really enjoy the talking portion, the other merely tolerates it to get her device. Often while her attitude is initially bad, she gets so caught up in the conversation she doesn't realize we're off the toll road. I call that a win!

It is noteworthy to mention at this point that even the best of children may try out the new habit of telling you things about the other parent or what happened at their house that creates an unhealthy reward cycle. What your intuitive child may consciously or subconsciously realize is that, if they give you the information they think you want to hear or if they ramp themselves up into an emotional state, you reward the behavior by giving them extra special attention that they crave to re-establish their sense of security. I just want to put that on your radar. Kids are smart.

The mind is a crazy amazing thing. It also supports why taking time to intentionally think and process all the things swirling around in your mind is so important. Consider getting in the habit of drinking a slow glass of tea before bed to encounter some of the swirling thoughts — feel the feels. Note that I say tea, not wine, because what I don't want you to do is numb the pain. Also let's face it, there isn't enough wine in the world to numb what you're feeling and it's a slippery slope. Remember Chapter 1? "If you're going through hell, keep going." You will get through this; you have a lifetime of surviving the hard stuff behind you. Maybe it's a good time to re-read that list to remind yourself of the other hard things that you've overcome or accomplished already.

By reading this book, you are actively tackling co-parenting and making your best effort to not only survive divorce but also thrive. In Chapter 10, we will discuss situations where a counselor might be helpful for you. For right now, we're focused on helping your kids survive and move towards thriving. Sometimes the reality is that they may need a counselor, too. This does not mean you are failing. You are a person trying your best to survive this hard season. One of the most common reasons kids need counseling in this period is that they need their own person who's not on a team and can offer healthy and unbiased feedback. What I mean by that is, whether real or perceived, they may be feeling in the middle.

Other times, you may see your "easy" child melting down because they don't want to burden you with their feelings. Their compassion for what you're going through makes them feel like they need to just suck it up or tamp it down to keep functioning so they don't make your life any harder than it already is. You can bless them with the gift of a counselor to help them process life right now. If you choose to do this, just figure who's on your insurance that sees children. A great question to ask the counselor is about how many clients they are currently seeing in your child's age range or related experience. If they say "none", call someone else. You want someone who has experience connecting with children your child's age. Their focus in counseling will likely be to just get them talking, guiding them through the grief process of divorce, and increasing their coping skills.

If your child has started acting out or you're seeing an increase in defiance, this is also a great time to seek out a counselor for them. Look for a counselor that may have been a school counselor previously and has a private practice on the side. One filter in your search will be their license type. Look for a Licensed Professional Clinical Counselor (LPCC or LPC depending on your state) rather than a Licensed Marriage and Family Therapist (LMFT). You may see they are an associate or intern rather than licensed. That's okay, as they are often younger and still hold a master's degree; it just means they are in their first few thousand hours of practice and must report to a supervisor. They might be slightly less expensive but are usually not covered by insurance. If you think the therapist might get pulled into your custody hearings, go with someone licensed.

Lastly, while we're focused on your child, let's talk about some somatic or physiological symptoms that you might see arise as a stress response to all the life changes. This one was hard on my mommy heart to admit. For my child prone to anxiety, it wasn't the first time I'd seen her get a legit tummy ache before doing something that made her nervous, but this time it felt like my fault. The thing to keep in mind is that *when you treat the feelings, many times the physical pain will go away.*

What does "treat the feelings" mean? I mean talk

about the emotions, normalize them, and show them how to cope. Big picture, this is a great skill for them to learn for life and will always serve them well. In the moment though, it's just sad.

The first step is distinguishing between pain based in biology (something wrong in your body), versus physiological (something wrong in your brain). Ask them, "Tell me about the pain." If when describing the pain they are using words that sound like they're describing anxiety, then it's probably a physiological response. For example: "Mommy, my tummy feels really jumpy."

Always ask about food and water, too. I can't even believe how many times my kids get headaches simply because they don't drink enough water throughout the day. It's honestly head-slamming painful when they are still making this mistake and they're in middle school. Or my personal favorite, when they realize this is the issue, drink a little cup of water and the minute they put the cup down they think the pain should go away. Oh man, I know it's normal, but it drives me batty.

Figuring out when the last time they ate was and what they ate can be an important factor, too. Specifically looking for whether they've eaten any protein in the last couple of hours. Often, food tends to affect emotions and energy levels, which are important. Recognize that your child may be tired when you pick them up in the morning from the other parent, not because the other parent let them stay up too late, but because they maybe didn't have any protein as part of their breakfast. You may want to future-focus a suggestion to the other parent in a simple email request, generously phrased along the lines of: "Hi Bob, when I picked up Johnny this morning, he seemed really tired. I know you're super busy getting ready for work in the mornings, too, but I was hoping you could encourage Johnny to eat some yogurt or other protein as part of his breakfast so he can function a little better as his morning proceeds. Just a request to consider, no need to respond. Thanks."

Back to physiological pain. So, you've realized that their headache is probably due to anxiety rather than dehydration, now what? Pause for a moment and recognize that your child is anxious. This is likely not your fault, nor the other parent's fault; it's about change. Change is easy for some kids and extremely difficult for others. Many children are somewhere in the middle of that adaptability spectrum, but if you have multiple children, it is likely that at least one struggles.

When we talk about anxiety, think of it as a response. In order to help your child's pain go away, you need to help them have a different response. I'm talking about coping mechanisms. Teaching your child that if they stuff their feelings, those feelings will ooze out in a different way. You don't need to have a big conversation regarding "why" they're having the feelings. In fact, that might make it worse. Teach them a different way to consciously process and respond to the feelings. I love to remind my kids, "It's okay to have every single feeling you have. You get to decide what you *do* with that feeling." This encourages a sense of control and empowers them.

What are appropriate things to do with our feelings? Think about changing their sensory experience. Anything related to touch, taste, smell, sight, or sound. Here are some examples:

TOUCH
Slime/playdough, massage your feet/hands

TASTE
Gum, mints, popsicle, sour candy, suck on ice

SMELL
Lavender, peppermint, lemon, favorite flower

SIGHT
Go outside, place a washcloth on eyes, focus on watching a candle burn

SOUND
Listen to music the opposite of your mood, find quiet, listen to nature, sound machine

For more ideas in a printable document to post on your wall check out my website: *Surviving2Thriving.life*.

I also really love art as an outlet, with the focus on creating, not the finished product. If you think of doing art as a faucet for your creativity, there is a wonderful freedom to release emotions in the process. I love coloring or drawing colorful geometric designs because it takes the pressure off "getting it right." A cheap set of watercolors and some computer paper is a great way to start. Often you will find the mood reflected in the color choices. Let them lead the talking. Maybe ask a few open-ended questions like, "Hey, is there anything I can do to make your day a little better?" or "Is there anything that you want to talk about?" and let them know that it's okay if they just want to paint or color in silence (like literally use words to say that). You can also ask if they want music on or off. Consider letting them choose what kind of music style goes with their heart; some good options are classical or calm worship music. Sometimes they prefer music with no words (instrumental). Give them lots of control in this activity. They are likely feeling like their world is out of control and you're trying to help them take it back. When they seem particularly angry and you're not really sure why, try handing them a balloon to blow up. When you push out more air than you breathe in, it calms down your parasympathetic nervous system. That may be way more info than you needed, but know there's science behind why this works really well.

Co-parenting, like regular parenting, has its own learning curve. Perfection is not the expectation.

Reality check: co-parenting in the early days will likely be a bit of a blundering mess. You're brand new to it, likely weren't expecting it, AND you're going through your own stuff! These are just some ideas and insights; do the best you can and that's good enough. Take heart, I didn't start where I ended up. So much of this is an unperfect process. You know what matters? That you're trying. Good job.

5

LIFE OVERHAUL

COOL SO NOW YOU'VE FIGURED OUT how you're going to help your kids survive. What about you? Where are you at? There's not a right or wrong answer. I just want you to self-assess. Seriously, take a second to think about how you are doing. Have you taken a shower today? Is it hard for you to wake up in the morning? Is it hard to go to sleep or stay asleep? Are you eating regularly? Are you being kind to your body? How's your hair? Are there bags under your eyes from crying so much? How's your work productivity? Have you seen or talked to your best friend this week? Like it or not, the answers are all indicators of how you're doing.

In the last chapter, we talked about helping your kids cope but what are you doing that's refreshing your spirit so that you'll survive another grueling day? I love routine. I know some people hate it, but for me and my squirrely brain, it brings a sense of calmness and tends to put me in line with the person that I actually want to be. If left to my natural inclinations, I probably would become totally unregulated, going to bed at two in the morning, sleeping late but not feeling rested, thrashing through my whole day, probably not eating well because I'm in a rush, not getting done what I wanted to get done at work or personally, not having enough time to work out, or feeling too tired. Blah — I'll be honest, it's one of the reasons I love that I have school-aged children; it forces me into a rhythm.

It starts with going to bed by a certain time so that I can successfully drag my butt out of bed on time to be the mom I want to be with my kids. It is important to me to set a positive tone for them before they go to school so that they get their day started off well. If I'm overtired and grumpy and have no patience to deal with my grumpy thirteen-year-old, I don't like that version of me! Rather than beat myself up for the end result (not being the mom I want to be), I have to trace my day in reverse and figure out where I can change my behavior to get a different result. The findings: I am a better parent when I get eight hours of sleep.

While I consider myself a very open-minded person and very much live by the "to each their own" model, I really think everyone needs exercise of some sort for their mental health. Simply put, it gets the yucky out. Now, what exercise looks like to you and how often you do it can have a million variations. At an absolute bare minimum, I would encourage you to move your body for at least twenty minutes, three times a week. That's a low bar and most of us need more than that, but maybe it's all that you can manage right now. I can respect that but encourage you to build on it.

I also love for one of my exercise activities to be outdoors. Man, I wish I loved biking; I just don't, and I've come to terms with that, even though I love the idea of it. Fortunately, I live close to the beach and find that a beach walk really refreshes me. I try to stay off my phone and don't even listen to podcasts. I try to just enjoy the moment and process life. However, I know outdoor exercise is not always feasible year-round based on where you live, so again, the theme is to figure out what makes sense for you.

This routine can pose a major childcare issue. Get creative! Maybe you do a yoga video before bed or wake up early a few days a week to squeeze in a workout video. Consider a kid swap with a friend to do a longer outdoor exercise while you take turns watching each other's kids. Maybe you figure out something to do with the kids; what about a hike together every Saturday? I know, I know, those little legs of theirs kill your pace, but it's still really great just to be moving. Or maybe while they stop to pick a flower, you drop down to do a burpee. Get it girl! That's enough to make me hate flowers, though. Maybe you used to swim in high school, so you start swimming at your local community pool. Maybe you join a city soccer team and make new friends. I guarantee that you're more likely to stick with it if it's something you actually enjoy doing.

When you figure out what exercise works for you, make a plan for when you will get it done. There's something about taking it from "I'm going to run this week" to making it specific and time locked. For example, I'm going to take a run Monday, Thursday and Saturday this week at 6 a.m. before the kids wake up. When you have a plan, you are so much more likely to stick with it. Write it on your calendar.

Yeah, you better have a calendar; a good old fashion paper one preferably. You can even display a whiteboard calendar somewhere in your house, depending on whether you want your kids to see it. Side note, having a printed custody calendar can help your kids plan better for transitions, both with their personal items and emotions. This can lead to a reduction in stress for everyone in your household. Stress causes brain fog and I think it's safe to assume that you're stressed! Help your poor, stressed brain out and give it the gift of a calendar or planner. It will also help you maintain your sense of competency to show up where you need to be, when you need to be there. And guess what? When you don't perceive yourself as a train wreck … it will actually help you not be a train wreck, yay!

I'm such a nerd; listening to podcasts is a way that I

refresh my soul. To some people, it might sound crazy, but I truly love learning. I love expanding my thinking or learning new information, in the same way that I love going to a professional conference. At the risk of sounding cheesy, what refreshes your soul? Really think about that for a moment. Sometimes a question like this can feel disingenuous, but I think it's important for you to pause and answer this. What makes you excited for life, heck, just excited to get up that day?

For some people, it's reorganizing things. For others, it's playing a musical instrument. For me, there was a point in my divorce when I was super busy juggling kids and work, then the kids would go with their dad, and suddenly, I had a whole evening free with no kids! This can be horrifying and wonderful in the same breath. More on that later in this chapter.

I have a friend who loves holding babies so much; that's probably her "thing" that refreshes her. Kittens may have that same effect on me. There is something that is wonderful about pets when you're going through hard stuff. I swear my cat has a special radar to detect when someone in our house is crying and goes to them! Anyway, find your "thing." If you're lucky, maybe it will be something active.

Once you find (or remember) what your thing is that refreshes your soul, plan to do it. Remember that calendar concept from earlier in this chapter? Just like you're scheduling exercise, figure out when you're going to make time to do the activities that fill you up so that you might survive another week. Depending on what your thing is, it may take more planning on your part. Maybe it's a Rachel Hollis or Freakonomics podcast on your way to work Tuesday and Thursday, or maybe it's stand-up paddle boarding with your kids after school on Fridays. Whatever it is, make time and schedule it. Notice I said *make time* not *when you have time*. Because the reality is that time slips away, especially if you're stressed out and spread thin. Trust me, I get it.

When you realize how refreshing this is, it will get easier to make it a priority. Sometimes you may need to find a more conducive idea to fit your current situation. Hint: It's likely that you have time on one end of your day. Either your kids are little and you have a small window between when they go to bed and when you go to bed, or they're older and you can wake up before them. Sometimes it can be as simple as taking time to stretch in the morning.

In the early days for me, I gave myself one hour to run around and do all the miscellaneous household things after I put my kids to bed. I prioritized my never-ending to-do list by what really needed to be done that evening. When the hour was up, I was dedicated to my "me time" and bumped the rest of the things I needed to get done to the following evening or weekend. If you don't take time off for you, the compounding effect of everything you're going through will bog you down. And it will happen so slowly that

oning 3ty seg

you may not notice until it gets really bad and looks something like depression.

I did something profound … I didn't turn on the TV during my "me time"! Okay, some of you are like, "how is that profound?" Others are like, "No way, you've lost your freaking mind. I need my Netflix!" For me it was profound because it was a habit that I'd gotten into with my ex-husband. What I'd forgotten through the years was that I actually don't like TV. Don't get me wrong, I can totally get sucked into a good show, but I created a habit of watching shows he found interesting just to be near him. Well, now he's gone! What are you doing out of habit that is a misuse of your time? Things that you did because they were habits of your spouses or compromises. Great in marriage, but … now you're not married, or almost not married. How many things did you do in marriage that you didn't like and even hated? I encourage you to take a moment and write a list. In fact, I'll make it easy for you. List three things right here that you did for, or with, your ex-spouse that you really did not enjoy. Seriously, take a moment to fill in the blanks!

1. _____
2. _____
3. _____

It's so important that we're going to dig in here, and it's going to get good. And no, you can't hold this list in your head. There are too many other things floating around in there and there's going to be a Step 2 to this list. Okay, now list them out and come up with at least three. Some of you may need a separate piece of paper to write an entire sheet. It's not a contest, just be real about it.

Was it hard? Did it feel good to see it all written down? Or maybe it pissed you off because you didn't realize that you were doing so much stuff you didn't like. Now brace yourself; look at your list. What can you eliminate now that you're not with that person, or how can you do it differently? Let me give you an example. One of the things I compromised on for eleven years was overcooked vegetables! One night after he left, as I was steaming broccoli it occurred to me … I can have crunchy-ish steamed vegetables again! Not to mention, we liked opposite vegetables in general, and for years I had been making the vegetables he preferred over the ones that I preferred. Let's be honest, one of the best things about being divorced is how little you actually cook these days, or that the meals can be far less complicated. I even got to a point where I missed cooking for adults. Fortunately, I had plenty of sweet friends willing to join us for dinner. I've even joked that my now husband just kept coming over because I kept feeding him, kind of like a stray cat. I even had another newly divorced friend whose ex-husband used to do all the cooking and wanted to learn; we enjoyed making meals together.

I swear, there are some perks about divorce. While they likely don't outweigh the bad, otherwise you'd still be married, it's nice when you realize these little things. I remember the moment my sister pointed out I never have to spend another holiday with my ex-husband's dysfunctional family! Cheers to undercooked vegetables and good riddance to my prior in-laws!

Speaking of cheers, one of the dumb things your friends might say in the early days is, "You're so lucky!" in response to your kids being with the other parent for the weekend. Bless them, they don't understand at all. Maybe it really will be like that eventually. While I've definitely gotten used to it and enjoy it now years later, it took me some time to come to terms with it.

To the married individual, time without kids when you're not at work may sound glorious. Honestly, I probably would have said the same dumb thing to a new divorcee, too. When you're on the front end of divorce, it's one of the many things that is different. If you're like me, it can feel like a gaping hole that is hard to figure out. I often was so busy juggling the majority of custody that I thought I needed to spend the time getting all the extra things done when my kids weren't around. Sometimes I moped around sad and shocked at this unanticipated path I was on. Other times, I went on little trips with girlfriends or hung out with friends or family. Whatever I did, it just felt weird, if nothing else.

I rediscovered in this phase the joy of wandering. I forgot what "life before children" was like — to not have a plan, to not think about what I needed to get done, but just to go to a cool area with no timeline and wander. If I saw something interesting, I could just pause and enjoy or wander down that path with no regard to an agenda. I could strike up interesting conversations with strangers. I love talking to people; I love hearing their stories. It's why I became a counselor … but I had forgotten this in the thrash of life.

However you decide to spend this time, I encourage you in the early days to: 1) plan it, and 2) feel the emotions. It may seem counterintuitive to tell you to plan it, despite the paragraph before saying how much I enjoy wandering, so let me explain. You can plan to wander by not planning other things. If your plan is to wander in downtown Laguna Beach at 2 p.m., then don't plan coffee with a friend at 3 p.m. Plan to not plan.

The second encouragement around kid-free weekends is to allow yourself to feel the emotions. *Don't beat yourself up about the gap between whatever you think you should be feeling and what you are actually feeling.* This can apply to everything in life, but let's hone in on its application for this new version of weekends. You might feel a lot of things and it might be one minute happy about the massive garage sorting you just finished, to the next minute ugly crying because the ice cream truck goes by, but your kids aren't home.

I want to pause here for a second. In this very real scenario, the ice cream truck is what us therapists call a "trigger" — loosely defined as a stimulating action or visual that results in an intense emotional reaction, usually negative. I want you to be aware of this concept and how frequent of an experience it is for you when recovering from your marriage ending. It is possible that you have so many triggers with memories attached that life can feel like a bit of a warzone. Sometimes, just recognizing what your triggers are can help take away their power. For me, one of those things was a specific pillow on my couch. So many times, I put this pillow on my lap with my ex-husband's head on it where I gently rubbed his head until he fell asleep, often leaving me trapped and out of reach of the remote while I was stuck watching his show I didn't like. When we were married, it really didn't bother me that much. It was one way that I showed him love. But now, I had a different filter and that pillow pissed me off just to see it! Long story short, the pillow had to go. What items in your house are negative triggers for you? Maybe there are a few needless items that need to be dropped off at your local thrift shop?

Sometimes your motivation to do something comes from *understanding what happens if you don't recognize and process your emotions*. A lot of times we parent like this, and the cause and effect are very apparent. However, emotion-stuffing is easy to do yet hard to realize the consequences, often for many years. As a counselor, I beg you to allow yourself to feel your emotions. Consider it a way to save money on future counseling! When you don't feel your emotions, you are more likely to suffer from low-level depression, generalized anxiety and even panic attacks.

A note on panic attacks: have you had one yet? You may have at least battled the onset of one. Given all the intense change, it's highly likely. If you have not, maybe you're lucky or have learned skills to deal with high levels of stress through the years. Either way, here are a few tips:

1. *Don't* repeatedly think, "Am I having a panic attack?" and focus on your symptoms. This is the worst thing you can do.
2. *Do* repeat your mantra from Chapter 1.
3. *Do* practice slow deep breathing. Personally, I like box breathing because it takes a lot of concentration. Breathe in through your nose five counts, hold five counts, breathe out through your mouth for seven counts, hold five counts. I know the seven count ruins the image of a box, but it's important to breathe out longer than in because it relaxes your sympathetic nervous system. Visualize moving around the outline of a square as you do each action.

Think of a panic attack like getting in a fight with

your brain. You must actively fight to keep your brain from flipping to "crazy brain" — the emotional mind that is no longer capable of rational thoughts. When you lose that battle, you will literally think that you are going to die. Just to state the obvious, it's not a battle that you want to lose. It's important to discuss with your doctor your specific symptoms, frequency and situation to make sure there are no other biological issues at play and whether medication may be beneficial.

One of the things that may be stressing you out is the struggle of the unending to-do list. You may find yourself busier than ever as you play the role of both Mom and Dad. Suddenly, you have to do all of the things you used to do, plus the stuff your spouse did, in addition to your new "part-time job" of all the legal paperwork that comes along with divorce. I know that remembering to take the trash cans out to the curb every Thursday night was one thing that I never thought about before. I quickly learned to set a reminder on my phone. I even set an alarm for when I needed to leave to pick my kids up from school. It might sound silly, but what I realized is that any time I can release my mind from the burden of trying to remember things I felt less stressed. Less stress is always a good option.

As you begin to rebuild your life, I want to raise your self-awareness in order to point your intentions towards practical behavior changes. It is always amazing to me how much small changes can really shift your life course. I encourage you to look at the post-divorce days as a refining process. In the same way metal is heated to get the impurities out, your life is being intensified to find the best version of you.

6

FRIENDS

THE GOOD, THE BAD, AND THE UNEXPECTED

THIS IS A HARD ONE. A lot of this book is about what I learned the hard way. How you navigate your friendships may vary. But I do know that when you go through hard situations, you realize who your true friends are. Sadly, you will realize that some friends aren't who you thought they were. Other times, you will have acquaintances rise up in a way that really deepens the relationship. You definitely need them, now more than ever, so be cognizant and you will get it figured out who's who.

While you may have been a great friend in the past, allow yourself to realize you're probably not one right now, and that's okay. It's your turn to be the one who's not okay. Look for the people who are pouring into you, not the people who are trying to pull all the juicy details of why you're getting divorced. Good friends just want to walk alongside you. You can tell them the details, but don't feel like you have to. If you feel like your friend won't accept, "I don't want to talk about it" or "I'm not ready to talk about it," they might not be the friend you need for this season.

You know how wedding ceremony tradition dictates that you sit on the right side if you're the groom's guest and the left side if you're the bride's guest? Sometimes divorce can feel like that with your friends. I say *sometimes* because I think it really depends on how you and your ex are getting along post-divorce. If you are getting divorced because you gently drifted away over the last ten years, or there's no big singular "reason" that triggered the end of your marriage, this may not be an issue. But if you are not getting along in a big way, the reality is that your friends are going to have to pick a side. Some may do this naturally, simply because they never really knew your spouse that well, or maybe the wives spent a lot of time doing playdates while their husbands were at work. Different dynamics lead to natural divisions.

Occasionally, you might find that you have that one couple that really liked both of you. They may not even support your decision to get divorced. While it can be easy to find this hurtful, I'm going to encourage you not to take it personally. Likely their inability to accept your reality has more to do with them and their story, than it does with you. For this person, I encourage you to just give them space to decide. Some-times how each partner chooses to live post-divorce helps them make their decision. For example, say your ex decides "yahoo, I'm free!" and starts living a lifestyle far different than the one they used to, that alone may be enough. It's not about winning or losing or justifying your actions, it's about being 100% you, knowing that other people's opinion of you is just that: their opinion. *You will find your people and they will love you as you are.*

Oftentimes in divorce, there is a common thread that one partner no longer desires to be married to that person because they are so tired of being someone they're not or trying to be someone that is really just not achievable. This can look a million different ways, but I've seen it time and time again in people's stories. As you make new friends and figure out or remember who the real you is, stay authentic. Make sure you're consistent and true to you. I'm not saying don't compromise. I'm saying if you don't like going to clubs on the weekends, then don't make new single friends that habitually go to clubs most weekends.

It's all a process. Sometimes you have to go to the clubs to remember who you are, and oh yeah, that's not your thing. Knowing these things about yourself takes self-awareness though. It takes engaging in thinking about your experiences, about who you are at the core and about what you want. I know that sounds like a lot in the early stages of divorce, however engaging in such activities are the very things that are going to get you out of your hole and moving forward. As you rediscover yourself, you will feel energized. I promise. If you don't yet, keep trying, you will.

Early on, I really struggled with wanting to justify my divorce to others. What I realized is that if they know me and know who I really am, they know that things were far worse than I ever told them. The person they know would never get divorced if it wasn't unbearable to the core. Eventually I shared with a handful of friends the details about the "why," but I never really trusted the friends who I felt like were questioning the truth of my story.

It was a red flag to me if I found myself feeling judged. That is a sign that your story is not safe with that person. If you must prove that you're making the right decision, they're not on your team. Give them space or consider letting that friendship go for now. If they judge you in the form of question, be ready to utilize this phrase, "I think you already have your mind made up about my situation, so I don't really want to talk about it anymore." Example: "Don't you think it's selfish to your children if you get divorced?" Yep, someone actually asked me that! Girl, it's time for some boundaries!

Boundaries can be hard to define and implement in this situation, but think of them like emotional fences in the same way that we have a fence around our house to keep us safe. The fence keeps unwanted people out, and those that feel comfortable with us just open the gate and come in. Just because they are comfortable to come in, that doesn't mean that sometimes we don't have to ask them to leave if they aren't respecting us. Before I really understood boundaries, I didn't always realize that I was letting people in further than I wanted or even intended. As Lysa TerKeurst so eloquently said in regards to boundaries in her book *Forgiving What You Can't Forget*, "Not everyone gets or deserves access to you, your life, personal space or energy."

It's kind of like when you're first dating. You have to figure out what you're okay with physically. Whether you want to keep things at just kissing, or maybe they can touch your private parts but only outside of your clothes. And just because you did it with one boy after dating a year doesn't mean that the next boy can pick up right where he left off on the second date. For some of us in dating, physical boundaries (or lack thereof), just kind of happened. We let the other person lead the way and decided where things would stop. Well, you're all grown up now. Cut that nonsense out and decide what is okay with you before you're in the heat of the moment!

One of the hardest things about boundaries is knowing when to set them and with whom. Let's talk about some indicators for when you might need a boundary. The most common indicator that you may need to set a boundary is if you get angry when recounting a conversation. Perhaps in the moment you were so shocked the person did/said whatever they did/said that you let it go. Sometimes letting it go is a perfectly fine idea, especially if you feel like it was unusual or out of character for that person. Just letting it go can be a result of our best thinking or the way we were raised, and that's a great skill a lot of the time. However, our best thinking gets us into some seriously messed up scenarios sometimes. Another indicator that you may require a boundary is the warm wash of resentment. If you set a boundary, you can avoid the resentment. It empowers both parties to change the course of the relationship. It's kind of like parenting the kid who wants a second cookie. The easy thing to do is to just give them a second cookie; sometimes that's okay, but often you have to kindly tell them "no," which is much more difficult.

In this new phase of life, I know that I am horrifically encouraging you to acknowledge your feelings and emotions. This is one of the choices that you get to make but you also get to decide what you do with your feelings. Remember, *you don't get to choose which emotions you have, only what you do with them*. When you feel some of those red flag feelings mentioned above regarding when to set a boundary: analyze it. What do you want to do with this feeling?

Setting a boundary goes something like this: "When you choose to _____ , I feel _____ . If you do _____ again, then I will _____ ." There are three keys. First, think about what you're going to say in advance. Second, don't set a boundary from a one-time violation. If you do that, you will lose a lot of friends because no one's perfect. And lastly, be specific about what action the other person is doing that is not okay. The second part of your statement above, "If you do _____ again then I will _____ ," is an action you will take to emotionally protect yourself (a.k.a. the fence).

For example, say every time you see your grandma the first thing out of her mouth after "hi" is a comment on your weight. Whether the comment is good or bad is irrelevant because you hate that the emphasis is on your weight. Now let's practice generously giving Grandma grace. Often people do their undesirable behaviors because they either don't realize the impact or they don't know an alternative behavior. In this example, you might consider saying something like, "Grandma, I love you to pieces. It would mean so much to me if when I first saw you, you didn't comment on my weight. It's really a struggle for me and even when I'm losing weight, I always feel like I should be thinner. Maybe instead, you could try asking me about work, or what I'm doing that's making me happy these days? These questions would be more helpful. I know you're well intended; it just hurts my heart to focus on my weight." Now Grandma is pretty old, so she's likely pretty stuck in her ways. Expect that she might justify her actions, deny them or just plain call you sensitive. That's her choice.

Here's where you get to make your choice. If she

chooses to acknowledge your feelings and says, "Oh, I'm so sorry, Sweetie, I will try that next time, but I'm old so you might have to remind me." Great! But if she justifies, denies, or shames you, you must be ready to emotionally move away. It might sound something like, "Okay, Grandma. I'm just trying to help our relationship be close, but when you continue to do things I tell you hurt my heart, I might not want to visit you as much." I know it's uncomfortable and awkward at best, but remember, your feelings count. *Other people's opinion of you is not more important than the hurt they cause you; it's not okay.*

This might be a no-brainer for some of you, but it may be profound for others: *your feelings are equally as important as everyone else's.* It sounds obvious on the surface but it can be really hard to actually believe and make your actions match. If you replace the word "feelings" with the word "time" in the above statement, it may be an easier way to self-evaluate. Your time is equally as important as everyone else's time.

When you're not getting done what you need to get done for you because everyone else's stuff is taking up your time, that's your fault … and your stinking thinking. By "need to get done" I'm not talking about pedicures ladies, I'm talking about when you haven't had your well check but your kids always manage to get theirs in their birth month. And just to further clarify, if you're like me and your kids don't get their well checks the month of their birth month, no judgement, I'm just looking for consistency ... I have a lot of grace for imperfect parenting because life is imperfect. I plan and make lists like a maniac because it's a lot!

I digress, boundaries can look a lot of different ways. Sometimes it looks like figuring out what you want to do different next time. Sometimes we stay stuck as the person other people know us as and the identity other people place over us. Now is a great time to break that. Let me give you an example.

Growing up, I was known as a leader; as a result, I planned many school events and social gatherings. I liked doing it but often I wished that I had some help or that someone else took a turn occasionally. I could never really figure out how to shift out of this role from the level I took on. However, after I had kids, I knew I wanted to make a conscious effort to make mommy friends who took some initiative to plan get-togethers. As a working mom of one, and shortly thereafter two little ones with a not-so-good (to put it lightly) marriage, I wanted my friends to help carry the load of coordinating social events. So I put a new filtering rule in place for my friendships. When I met a potential mommy friend, I'd plan the first playdate then make sure they had my number and enthusiastically let them know I'd really love to get together again. Then I'd wait for them to contact me. Oh man, this was not easy for me; patience is not my virtue. I'm a person who likes to make things happen, I'm a planner ... and I had to wait on them. Some never reached out, some took way longer than I would have liked and some did it right away. The point is, I figured out one thing I needed to shift in my friendships as a whole and I made a rule for myself to essentially screen out people that didn't meet this criterion. You can look at it like maybe I missed out on a lot of good friendships, but I look at it like I figured out one little area I needed things different and connected the dots to get there.

What is helpful from friends when you're going through divorce? HELP! Like literally, physical help. If you're the one who stayed in the family house, you're now the one doing all the things that were shared between two people previously. If you're moving, getting re-settled, and furnishing a place from scratch — that's a lot of work! You probably have friends that think that sounds fun; let them help you. Go so far as getting them a list and a budget. The right person will be very excited to help you with this task. Sometimes it's something as simple as asking a mom friend from your kid's school to have your child over every Wednesday after school. It's a practical way that you can free up some time to squeeze in a big hike to mentally prepare yourself to survive the rest of your week and get some of your frustration and negative energy out.

Be ready to offer specific ways your friends can help. I found that a lot of well-meaning friends would say, "Let me know what I can do to help" and I would just respond with, "Okay." But here's what I learned: if

TORREY COMMISSO

I had a few easy things I could throw out for options they were much more likely to make that offer a reality. Occasionally, people maybe didn't have the intention to put the offer into action; if that's the vibe you sense after throwing out a few options, consider tacking on the phrase "if you want to think about it and let me know over text that's fine, too." It takes the pressure off in the moment, or if they're like me they may need to go home and look at their calendar to figure out what works best.

If I'm honest, I am the worst at asking for help. Or at least I was. Divorce broke me — for the better. I spent my life up to that point not letting people in. I'd been hurt too many times, and the vulnerability of letting someone help me came with the horrifying consequence of being dependent on someone else. I loved to help other people though; I loved to be needed. This is another example of my best thinking getting me into a huge mess.

There is a healthy balance. What I've realized is: there is a very good and healthy version of this that I get to use as a therapist and in all my current relation-ships; it just involves a lot of self-awareness and bound-aries, or I get taken advantage of. If you're like me and you struggle to let people help you, my sister explained it to me so well when she said, "You need to *give* people the opportunity to help you." She went on to explain that when I reverse the situation and I help someone else, whether big or little, it genuinely brings me joy.

76

I'm in a stage of life when those close to me see and know I'm struggling, it is important for me to offer them the opportunity to lighten my load a little. It's a way for them to find a little joy in their day. I knew she was right, and I could do that.

You might have some ideas about what friends should and shouldn't be doing. The counselor in me would like to encourage you to gently let those things be known. Don't assume anything about your friends. I found that some of the most well-intended friends did dumb things, not because they were jerks, but because they just had no idea. Unless you've gone through divorce, it's a very unique hardship/trauma; don't expect people to know what to do or say. Sometimes just having an open conversation with them about what is and what is not helpful can make all the difference.

Notice I said *gently* let those things be known. Watch your words; you will need good friends in the coming days so try not to piss them off. Start with recognizing their effort. Try to see their heart in the situation and what might be hard for them. In fact, ask them what's hard for them about your situation. Maybe they really liked your husband, and even if they understand why you're divorcing him, recognize they likely had their own separate relationship with your ex-spouse. Maybe you guys were a double couple and your best friend and her husband were best friends with each of you individually. Your divorce might be causing problems in their marriage because she's taking your side and her husband is taking your ex's side. This is totally a thing! A real bummer thing! But it's not your thing to take on. I just want you to recognize that your divorce can have an unintentional impact on your friends.

Another way I saw friends respond as an odd reaction to my divorce was that my choice to get divorced was taken as a personal affront to what they were choosing to do in their marriage. For some, it's like Pandora's box had been opened and if I was getting a divorce maybe they should, too. For me, these were the friends that had been walking the hard journey of marriage with me, ones that were in a similar situation to me; they were married to an addict, too. That if I was "giving up" (a.k.a. choosing to no longer tolerate his drug use, amongst other things) in my marriage that all of a sudden they were also considering not tolerating their spouse's behavior either. Perhaps the more fascinating response was the friends who continually tried to justify to me why they're still with their spouse. I found the latter response interesting because I would be talking about something in my life, and all of a sudden they would jump in to justifying their choice. Give them grace, listen to them just like I'm sure they've done plenty with you, then just stay in your lane and don't give advice. With one friend, I eventually had to confront this continual pattern. I told her, "Just because I chose to leave really has nothing to do with whatever you decide to do in your marriage. I hope you don't feel judged by me for staying." And I sincerely meant it!

In the same way you want people to respect your choices, you need to respect their choices. Whether it's your career path, hair color, car, or the way they parent — it doesn't matter. Their choices are just that, their choices. And your choices need to be equally respected even if they don't agree. Hopefully this isn't a deal-breaker in the friendship, but also know that it might be. As much as it can be a big blow to lose a friend, now more than ever, you need people who are 100% behind you.

One theme you might experience with friends is that they feel like they can't talk about their struggles because they're "too insignificant" compared to what you're going through. Sometimes they might drop little hints, or you might notice, "I don't really know how any of my friends are doing" … that means you've been doing all the talking. While it's fine to be the main talker with all the change and heartache you're likely going through, in order for your friendships to not wither and die, make sure you're taking time to still listen. Provoke the conversation even if it goes something like, "Even though I'm going through hard stuff I still want to be a good friend to you." Possibly insert an apology if maybe you've been doing all the talking or when they call, consider saying, "I'll be happy to tell you how I'm doing but first will you update me on what's going on with you?" They will appreciate this and it's likely easier for them to talk about the details of their life as significant if they go first. *Healthy friendships should always go both ways.*

What about the friends you don't want to talk about it with? You know, the mom-squad at school or colleagues at the office. You just don't want to peel back the layers, whether for professional reasons or to protect your kid's privacy, and you feel that little grimace as they gently pry for information. Again, I would like to reiterate: this is your story to tell or not tell. You decide — not "you answer anyone and every-one's questions until they stop asking." A great little prefabbed answer can come in really handy in those moments.

For example, a colleague walks up, "Hey, I heard you're going through a rough divorce. What'd he do?" It's very easy to vent in these moments and share what I will call an "inappropriate" amount of information. I will encourage you to swap in your prefabbed answer in that moment and call your best friend or therapist later. A prefabbed answer might go something like, "Yeah, it has been rough, but I don't really want to talk about it right now." Most people will respect that and oftentimes you'll learn that this acquaintance may be reaching out because they have some experience with divorce, whether it's them or a close friend or family member. They could be a good source of support, but just make sure you're not emotionally barfing on everyone who asks you how you're doing. Figure out who your people are.

DivorceCare can be a great place to make new friends in a similar chapter of life. This low-cost, nationwide support group network is usually held in churches, and it gives so much education and tools for going through divorce. It's always led by someone who is further down the road of surviving divorce and can add wisdom to the storm you're in.

You will lose friends. I know it sucks. I don't care how awesome you are or what your ex did or what's going on now, for so many different reasons you are likely to lose friends because you're going through a divorce. Everyone I've ever met going through a divorce can validate this harsh truth. I just want to put it on your radar so it feels a little less personal to you when it happens. Recognize it as part of the process. You will also make new friends and grow friendships deeper.

As I mentioned early in the chapter, a lot of these lessons I learned the hard way. I want to share two notes on friendship that I didn't anticipate. The first phenomenon that I didn't anticipate in my supporting relationships was how no one, literally no one, knew how bad my marriage was and they were hurt that I didn't let them in on my struggle when I was in it. On top of dealing with my own stuff, I had to recognize that as the truth came out about my marriage, *the people closest to me felt deceived.* On one hand, I can justify it. I let them know that he always threatened that if I told anyone about what was going on in our marriage then we were done. Literally I heard that again and again and my best of intentions just wanted to be married to him, to *make* our marriage work ... until I realized I alone couldn't *make* our marriage work; it was big time broken. But that's a whole other thing. The point is, my friends had no idea about the nightmare I had been stuck in for years. Not my best friends, not my sister, not my parents ... no one! I think it helped them to realize none of the others knew either, but the reality is they were hurt. And honestly that's on me; I could help them understand my dilemma, and they, being the wonderful people they are, all chose to forgive me, but it hurt them and it took time. Ultimately, they were sad for me that I was stuck in that alone but realized it wasn't about them. I learned a lot from that about letting people in on the hard stuff. It was one of those post-divorce growth moments where the hurt made me a better person moving forward. Perhaps there is something that happened in your marriage that has left unresolved wounds with friends. Maybe you had to miss someone's wedding because of a situation or dynamic within your marriage. Maybe your ex-spouse saw throwing baby showers as a waste of money and you still feel bad that you never offered this to your best friend. I don't know what your things might be, but I'm guessing there might be one and I encourage you to revisit it even if you think it's long in the past. It will bring peace and healing to your soul and your relationships.

I realized for my sake, to be my best self, I need to always let "my people" in on the hard stuff. If I can't tell them, then that was a red flag for me! David Feldman led a great body of research around a term he coined: "Post Traumatic Growth." We've likely all heard of Post-Traumatic Stress Disorder (PTSD), but I like the term Post Traumatic Growth. If you let it, this can be part of your story for the choices and the mindset you are approaching life with right now. Essential to the term "Post Traumatic Growth" is the recognition that first and foremost, you wish that the trauma didn't happen (in our case, divorce). It's not belittling the emotional pain and stress you are enduring currently, but recognizing it AND choosing to grow from it.

You are building your list from Chapter 1 of things you have survived. I can tell you if your divorce story is anything like mine, that time and time again this chapter of life becomes a reference point for relative pain. The more hard things you go through, the better you get at handling other hard things. Note that I didn't say easier. Just raising your competence. Also, it puts things in perspective. Things that you used to think were a big deal may not seem like such a big deal anymore. Maybe what qualifies as a bad day in the past may not be what qualifies as a bad day in the future.

The last observation on friendships I encountered

were the friends who questioned what they should have done differently so things didn't turn out the way they did for you. This has more to do with them and likely their codependent tendencies than you. To this I say, release them of the burden of this thought. The short answer is: nothing. They could and should have done absolutely nothing different because it's not their life; it's your life to screw up. Seriously, like you can say it jokingly or seriously, but it has so much truth. You can point out that even if they had seen something and wished they said something, the reality is that you may not have listened. There is no need for them to beat themselves up. Just let them know you appreciated that they've walked and continue to walk the journey of life with you; that's what you've always appreciated and continue to appreciate. *Perfection in relationship is never the expectation; communication is key.*

Wow, that was a lot. Friendships are complex and wonderful. As you weed through your friendships and how your time is spent, I know your relationships will go deeper. Some believe we are on this earth for the simple reason of relationships; I think there is truth in that. Good friendships in difficult times can make all the difference.

7

UNSHARING

UNSHARING — I made up this word, and I quickly came to love it, because I think it so accurately describes what the court calls "dividing assets". However that term doesn't embody all that I'm going to cover in this chapter. While we can laugh at this term, it's really not funny at all. We're talking about drawing a line down EVERYTHING not attached to you, including your precious children! Anything and everything that is outside of your body. Many of those things aren't about their material value but their priceless value and memories. Some of the things are from memories you have together, like that cute coffee mug you got in Hawaii on that great vacation together. Now you don't know whether to smash the coffee mug (ask him if he wants it) or treasure it as one of the few good memories you had left with him. This chapter is written to help you intentionally navigate this process.

Even your good memories can feel like all the color was drained from them. If there was infidelity or addiction that contributed to the end of your marriage, or a variety of other reasons, you may be viewing *all* your memories through a new lens — a lens that is not rose colored. I don't really have advice here other than just *acceptance*. It just is. In Dialectical Behavioral Therapy (DBT) we have a fancy name for this concept of "radical acceptance," meaning you are *intentionally* accepting the issue at hand. Interestingly, when I looked up the definition of "radical," I was expecting results related to slang use of the word common in the 80's. However, what I found was quite different. "Radical" is used to describe the other end of the spectrum from the typical-thinking or simply, "far-reaching." You don't need to wallow in the "why me," just acknowledge it's one more element to what you're going through — you will get through; keep walking.

One tidbit of wisdom I would offer here is to be careful what you break or burn. One of the items that really had me feeling all the emotions was my wedding dress. I loved this beautiful fluffy dress from the moment I laid eyes on it twelve years prior. It was everything I dreamed of, and I loved that it was totally inappropriate for my small and fairly casual wedding. It signified one of the few parts of my wedding that wasn't a compromise unlike so many of the other elements of our day. At the same time, with this new lens of realizing so many things about my marriage were lie on top of lie, I was angry. A friend sent me some photos from Pinterest of trashing your wedding dress photo shoots post-divorce. It's a real thing, look it up! It's pretty funny (gone psycho at times … don't light your wedding dress on fire while you're wearing it!!!). Maybe some variation of this appeals to you as an option. For me, in the end, that beautiful dress is boxed up in my closet next to my second wedding dress. I have two girls; those dresses are two dresses that represent me and what I wanted. I choose not to let my bad marriage ruin one of those beautiful dresses.

On the other hand, I opted to get rid of all my lingerie no matter how pretty it was. It just didn't feel right even when I gave it time. Eventually I got a new mattress and bedding. For me and my story it was just an ick factor, yeah that's totally a scientific term! These are just examples; you have to figure out what things trigger you. I hope you don't trash it all, though. For the items that just feel too "hot," I say box them up in the garage or at your parent's house and decide later when emotions are not running so high.

The hardest thing to figure out what to do with was pictures! If you're anything like me, they're all over your house. I am blessed by having an amazing family photographer for a sister. There were so many non-posed pictures of our family that previously brought joy to my heart to see throughout my days. Those cute little toddler and baby faces — love them. And now they were like a slap in the face to what isn't.

So what do you do? I had no idea. Early on I wanted to take each one down and huck it over the fence into the vast open hills behind our house (I did try this with one item, I can say it went way better in my head). Family photos is one way I encourage you to rise up and be mature for your kid's sake. Let them have good memories of your intact family — let them cherish those. Just because they might be ruined for you, don't you dare ruin those memories for them ... not cool. So no drawing on Dad's face with a sharpie, putting a sticker or your favorite celebrity cutout on top of his image ... no matter what. I don't care what they say or how they may react to your face. This will screw up your kids and cause them emotional distress.

As you take pictures down that you very well may never want to see again, consider putting together a bag or box for each of your children to divide them up for them and let them decide whether to keep them. What about the wedding album? Which of your kids might really cherish it? If you're not sure, just box it up. It may be too soon to decide. You can get rid of some or even a lot of photos, but I just strongly encourage you not to get rid of all of them.

A note on negotiation, let me be clear: this is not legal advice, just simply some negotiating tips if you're trying to figure out what you want your attorney to fight for or what requests you want to come to the table with, you may find this next section helpful. Before I was a therapist I worked in commercial real estate. And before that I was a little sister and family peacekeeper. I've learned a few things about negotiation through the years.

Tip #1 – Aim high. I don't care how much of a straightforward, no B.S. person you are, never come to the table asking for only what you want. Recognize that this process depends on both parties compromising. If you show up only asking for the things you want, know that you're not going to get all of them. Put on your best poker face and over-ask knowing you're going to be "giving up" items. Ask for the things you know he's going to really want, not because you want them, but because he's going to be willing to give up more to get those things.

Tip #2 – Prioritize what you want. Make a list and, no matter how silly it seems, put what matters to you in all realms. My attorney was awesome enough to point out that you can't trade parenting time for assets in court … just saying, think about it. Get creative and encourage him to figure out what he really wants, too. Maybe you have a tradition around a holiday and that you really want to always have the kids on Valentine's Day, and he wants them for every Spring Break. There's no wrong way to do this — no I take that back there is, never threaten violence even if you don't intend to act on it. I just want you to think about it. Maybe he gets the dog, and you want the cat. Maybe you decide to switch cars. Maybe you carve out some random little custody time for the other parent so you can make it to book club the first Thursday of every month without having to pay a babysitter. Maybe he doesn't want his Saturday custody time to start until noon so he has time to do a big hike before the kids join him for the weekend. It does not all have to be lose/lose.

Tip #3 – Leave the past out of it. Try as best as humanly possible, it's truly a big ask, to contain your emotions in this process and to view it more of a business transaction. Again, this takes a lot of emotional maturity. It's very easy to want to name call when they're not giving you what you want. If you stand on the cliff of "I deserve this" … you probably won't get it. If you can try to approach it in a "what if you get _____ and I get _____" approach, you will likely have much more luck in your negotiations. Now because you were just married to this person, you likely know what is near and dear to their heart (and vice versa), so keep that in mind. When they're asking for the items you know are dear to their heart, don't settle at a financially valued equivalent. A good negotiator will use these items to get what they really want, too, even if it's worth more money.

Okay so maybe after reading those tips you either think I'm a big jerk and you're not even sure you can finish the book, or you think I'm brilliant and I just saved you thousands in attorney costs. Whichever it is, I hope you keep reading and I'll get back in my lane and stick to the issues of the heart and mind. *The whole underlying purpose of this book is to empower you to make a series of choices that are right for you.*

As you unshare your life, we must discuss your home. Does it still feel like home or is it just a house where you live? Maybe by this point you've both moved out. I know this step, at whatever point it comes, is always hard for everyone emotionally, and sometimes physically if you have to move locations.

We already talked about pictures but what are the things in your house that bring you down? What have you always wanted to do to your house that either he wouldn't let you or you just weren't quite sure? For me, I realized that I actually wanted a whole lot more color in my house. My ex thought some of the "color pops" I tried out were too much, but the house always felt a little blah to me. Well now it was my house, so I added some new colorful pillows to my tan couch and changed some artwork out where there were family pictures before. I picked up a new tablecloth and even started cutting a few greens from my backyard to put in a mason jar on the table. I got rid of a lot of clutter on the counters and I started tacking sayings and bible verses around my house that encouraged me. My house had a whole new vibe that really inspired me rather than the "blah" adding to my struggling sadness. This phase is hard enough; you don't need your house to kick you while you're down.

What else in your life is too much? What can you cut? Maybe it's the perfect time to stop going to PTA

Meetings — divorce is a great excuse. Maybe you want to start going to PTA Meetings, and he used to want you home with him and the kids in the evenings. Maybe there's a hobby you did with your spouse just to spend time with them, but you didn't actually like it that much. Well guess what? He's gone now so go ahead and OfferUp your tennis racket or golf clubs. You're free! Doesn't matter what it is, I just want you to think about what you want now that he's not a factor.

Eventually I decided I wanted a different life, and it didn't include that house. I wanted a smaller house, like a home base. As my kids grew up and I got more into my career, we really weren't home that much but I sure spent a lot of time cleaning it. I found myself out of the home a lot. I was being active and social — I liked it! I realized I wanted a fresh start. Everyone knew me as "the one who got divorced." I didn't want that to define me. I finally stopped explaining it and realized nobody really cared; no explanation was needed. I was also trying to spend as much time at the beach as I could as I realized it refreshed my soul. I wanted to build a life I didn't feel the need to vacation from. So I moved forty miles away to a house half the size. I'd loved that city for years but could never convince my ex-husband to move there because of his commute. I couldn't believe the weight that was lifted when I got out of that house. Changing the décor was not enough to shed the memories that haunted me there. Maybe you don't feel safe in a house anymore; maybe a condo or apartment is more appealing. I'm not saying this is a solution for everyone, or even an option, I just encourage you to be aware of how you feel about your house. For some, it doesn't bother them at all; good for you, that's much easier!

At the end of unsharing all your stuff, you really do need to take time to celebrate. Many couples spend months and even years in this step of divorce. It's really, really hard and emotional for so many reasons. My dad used to tell me, one sign of a good compromise is BOTH sides are mildly unhappy with the results. While I don't love this, I think there's a lot of truth to the statement. Don't expect you're going to get everything you want. If it only took days or weeks to come to terms in your negotiation you need to especially celebrate that! Unsharing is no fun and one of the really crappy parts about the getting divorced process. All I can encourage is intentionality.

8

WHEN "CHOOSE JOY!" PISSES YOU OFF

IF YOU'RE LIKE ME and the most well-meaning women around you encourage you to "Choose joy!", refrain from punching them in the face or dusting off your explicit vocabulary. Viola! There's your emotion, note it, then choose what you do with it. Often my best option was to paste a fake, forced smile on my face and try to get away. I cringe a little at encouraging you to be fake because one of my highest values is showing up authentically, but sometimes you just have to pick your battles. The reality is that some people just don't get where you're at and you don't need to spend the energy helping each and every person understand. Let your takeaway be recognizing they were well-intended and fortunate that they have no realm of knowledge for the hell you are currently walking through.

You will have to fight for your sanity in divorce. Since we're all parents here, I feel that a good Unikitty reference from *The Lego Movie* is in store. If you haven't seen this movie, it's great and I encourage you to engage in a movie night with your kids of all ages. There is humor for all ages in this movie and so many great messages that get thrown in. Unikitty — I love her so much! I kind of think she may be the embodiment of the falsehood of toxic positivity. In one of my favorite scenes, she is introducing Cloud CooCooLand, where there is "no frowny faces or negativity of any kind" amongst other humorous things. You will see Unikitty's struggle unfold in the movie as she struggles to stay positive in all circumstances. Eventually (I'm sorry I'm going to ruin this part of the movie for you) she flips. There is a time for anger, and she puts it into action to be a force for good.

My hope is that you don't let all the negativity ruin you; I'm here to tell you it can if you let it. What I want to be clear on is that your worst option is to tamp negative emotions down and pretend like they're not there. Poor Unikitty tried that: "Those we push down deep inside where you'll never ever, Ever, EVER find them!" That wasn't sustainable for Unikitty and it won't be for you either. It didn't work and it never does. If you want to be the best version of you, you must deal with your crap.

Get a counselor. It's too much for a friend to process with you. There are things that a friend can absolutely help with that we'll touch on in Chapter 9, but the depth of this agony is best sifted through with a professional. While journaling is good, and I hope this book helps you a lot, your story and the "whys" are unique. I don't care how awful your ex was, you picked them to spend your life with! Marriage is a relationship and a dance — a dance we learned from our parents and the people that surrounded us in childhood. While the circumstances leading up to the end of your marriage may not have been your fault, you had something to do with how it got that bad.

Before you throw the book across the room, please know that I say the hard things with the best of intentions to help you become the best version of you. I speak truth even when it's hard; it is a fine art to do it gently in a way you might hear me, so here's me trying. This might be the hardest part of this book to read. I truly believe part of your post-divorce recovery process is going to include some analysis so you don't repeat the same mistakes again. That while the final straw of your marriage might clearly land on your ex-spouse, a lot led up to that. If nothing else, consider the question: "Why did they think they could _____ and get away with it?" Were they doing it to hurt you intentionally? I'm going to tell you "likely not" ... but why weren't they thinking about the impact? How many other times did they do hurtful things and you never spoke up? Did you place too high of a bar that they couldn't possibly live up to? Did you speak up for what you wanted to be different in the marriage? If so, was it just at the very end? How many years did you accept hurtful things that in hindsight really were not okay with you? Was it "your" house and kids to take care of instead of a shared responsibility? Who modeled that to you? How was your marriage like your parents' marriage? If you could change just one thing about your ex-spouse, what would it be?

On the surface, everything in my story felt "not fair." Well, as I yelled at my children one day while they bickered in the backseat about something dumb, "LIFE'S NOT FAIR!" And I hate that. I want so bad for life to be fair. It's not. If I'm honest, this probably works in my favor a ton of the time. In my life, I know I am blessed beyond belief, but when I isolate bits and pieces of my story, I can make an argument for "not fair." I think we all can. *But I choose to be grateful.* Joy and gratefulness are different. Sometimes joy during suffering feels impossible. But gratefulness during pain is difficult, though not counterintuitive to heartache. There is always something to be grateful for. There may not always be something to be joyful/happy about. I choose a growth mindset that keeps me believing that I can endure big things and be better because of the hard things. *If my life were easy, I wouldn't be the person I've become.* That's my soapbox for "Post Traumatic Growth."

If nothing else, dig deep to deal with your stuff because I swear, if you don't, you will end up repeating your mistakes. If you don't think you made mistakes, which I guarantee you did, then how are you possibly going to avoid doing them again? Let me give you a very real example from my story that opened my eyes to this possibility.

To keep this man anonymous, I'm not going to say how I met him, only that there was a single dad I met that I struck up easy casual conversation with regularly. As the casual conversation seemed to be migrating towards a time to hang out just the two of us (and I'll be honest I was very attracted to him), I listened and asked questions to get some more background information. What I learned was he had been mandated to treatment after more than one DUI, was currently in anger management classes, had very little contact or relationship with his kids, and his attitude around all of it was that it wasn't really a big deal and he didn't really have any issues. And these are only glimpses of what he told me as a friendly stranger! Maybe all those things are fine with you, but for me, this sounded very familiar to what I was running from and quite possibly worse. So that was my "ah-ha" moment — I need help. It's so crazy to me that I would be drawn to such a similar guy among all the other options. I had a type, and I desperately wanted to change it.

Don't do it for your next marriage; do it for you. *You have to get "you" right before you can attract a different, healthier person.* On that note, can you please use all your self-control and not start sleeping with anyone yet? Think of it like damage control. Sleeping with anyone right now is only going to make things worse in the long run.

I know, I KNOW, it's so hard — so hard. Married, good, regular sex … then nothing for over three years! Oh man, I joked with my best friend at six months post-divorce, "I don't know if I would have gotten divorced if I realized I'd have to go this long without sex." I seriously did not think of that aspect. I'll be honest, I love sex; I truly enjoy it with the right person. But now is not the time when you are recovering from divorce.

If ever there was a time to "self-indulge," it's now. If you're hesitant here, think of it as an investment in your future sex life, a different form of self-exploration. Just to be clear, yes, I am talking about masturbation. It's a great time to figure out yourself, in *every* aspect. If you have hang-ups about this because you were raised in 90's church purity culture, go re-read the relevant scripture. When you put it in context, you're fine. This message was approved by my pastoral counselor. I mean, if you can't be real with your counselor, then who can you be real with? I'm not lying when I say I understand this struggle. I had three people give me vibrators my first post-divorce birthday — my people know me! I say this to make it clear, I'm not one of those non-sexual women who is fine to abstain from sexual activity. I'm saying it's really freaking hard, but find a way!

While I want you to abstain for your own well-being, you can also understand this idea in the context of doing it (or more specifically "not doing it") so you don't hurt other people. Have you ever heard the saying, "hurt people, hurt people"? It's so true! The reality is you are healing right now. If you don't want some jacked up scar from this, then you need to refrain from sex while you get yourself right. It can be tempting to prove to yourself that you're still desirable, but now is not the time and that's got to come from the inside. If you need to prove through sex that you're going to bounce back from this, you're on the wrong track and this book probably isn't for you. Or maybe you've never been with anyone but your spouse. Well to that I say: you've practiced self-control before, so let's do it again. Maybe you were stuck in a sexless marriage for years — you're used to it; let's wait to celebrate.

In fact, let's use a recovery model to illustrate the importance of this horrible truth. When people first enter recovery, it is commonly recommended that they not only completely stop using whatever substance is the issue but also anything else that might serve a similar mind-altering purpose. This concept quickly became easy to prove because the swapping to an alternative was easy to see from a research standpoint based on hospital records. Stopping one unhealthy relationship just to replace it with another is not going to help you on your path to wellness. You have to get "you" right first before you can join up with someone else.

I'm going to tell you a secret, abstaining isn't about just "not doing it," it's about shifting your focus. If you're focused on not having sex, goodness gracious I feel ya, but I'm here to tell you that I figured out a better way of living. *Not having sex is about shifting your energy elsewhere; it's about focusing on what you really want and who you want to be.* When you step into that identity, it will get easier to make choices in line with that. Not easy, easier.

With my clients, all of them, there is always an ongoing conversation about coping. Good news, everyone finds different ways to cope. Bad news, often at least some of those ways are not healthy. I mean let's be honest, drinking a glass or two of wine is so much easier than going for a run. But I want you to consciously fight the urge of unhealthy coping, to view it as just that, unhealthy. Through this phase of life you are faced with so many choices; you have the opportunity again and again to stay on that path that will make all the difference in your future but in no way is it the easy path. *It is worth it.* I can't stress this enough — it is worth it for you and for your kids. I want you to live your best life because you want to; only you can walk this path out one choice at a time.

To that I say, "Chin up buttercup!" Keep your eyes on the horizon, not all the garbage going on now. The alternative is getting stuck in your very own hell on Earth. That might seem like an overstatement, but I honestly don't think it is because I have seen it.

You might have every reason in the world right now for people to feel bad for you. It can feel really nice to be coddled, especially coming out of a very hard marriage. Whether you left or whatever they did, it's so much change! I'm sure you will have days, heck, weeks even, where it feels like too much to get out of bed … but you did, and you will keep on because the alternative is way worse. The staying in bed, the drinking a whole bottle of wine by yourself, the sleeping with a stranger does not put you on the path to where you want to go. The easy thing is to get stuck: stuck in the wallowing, stuck in the mourning, stuck in the fighting, stuck in people feeling bad for you. Stop punishing yourself; dig deep and do it different. Let your path inspire other people. I love Mel Robbins' quote, "You have been assigned this mountain so that you can show others it can be moved."

I'm not trying to glamorize divorce in any way. I called it my best-worst option; when all I had left were a handful of crappy choices, divorce was the pick of the litter. It was not a path I wanted nor ever dreamed I'd be on. As much as my ex had threatened it and I thought it was only a matter of time before he left me, I was waiting for the day he did. It literally never even occurred to me to be the one to provoke it by drawing a line for what I wasn't okay with.

It took a nurse, my boss and a pastoral counselor to convince me to draw that line! And even when the pastoral counselor got me to the point of drawing that line, I wanted to believe that she was wrong. That when push came to shove, he would choose me. He didn't and I began to question everything. Those early weeks were the worst. For me, my faith made all the difference. It was my first glimmer of hope that I might survive this. There were so many "coincidences" I knew it couldn't possibly be by chance; they were too big.

I saw it first in my finances, maybe because God knew this was heavy on my heart. Here's the truth: when I asked my ex-husband to leave, I wasn't convinced he would. I was prepared to walk away from everything — I just wanted my kids and car. That wasn't how my story went and I'd love to ask God one day, "Why'd you bless me?" It started in small ways when unexpected money rolled in small amounts and unanticipated ways. The harder I leaned into God, the more He made the way.

For me in the early phase, I had to face my own judgement. I was the worst; I'm embarrassed to admit how I viewed other women who went through divorce … before that became my path to walk. Suddenly, I had so much grace for the choices that anyone and everyone made. I realized I had no idea what their story was no matter how well I thought I knew them. Even now, when strangers open up to me, I'm quick to insert a disclaimer: It's not my place to judge because I've learned — truly learned — it's absolutely not my place to judge. That my opinion is just that, my opinion.

There is something so much greater than all of us orchestrating this universe; I have no idea what role you will play as you interact with people throughout your life. I strongly believe we're here for relationships. *Life is too short not to say the hard things, and pour out grace and love to those we hold dear.* Life, especially right now, is so incredibly hard, but your story is not over. Right now, your story continues one painful step at a time. I encourage you, whatever your faith, *lean in.*

Lean in, not on your own understanding but in faith that you are part of something bigger. That *your pain has purpose, purpose that will make this world a better place.* I never thought in a chapter called "When 'Choose joy!' Pisses You Off" I'd be sharing my faith, but I guess that's consistent with who I am and how I work. I market myself as a Christian counselor. Clients must opt-in in order for me to use that counseling style, and inevitably many who have opted-in use swear words. They think because I'm a Christian that this is going to be offensive. It's not; swearing is never offensive to me when it's used authentically to express deep emotions. My goal is always for everyone in my life to be able to put all of themselves on the table. That's how we connect, when we're really seen just as we are, not how we want to be. That's the absolute opposite of perfectionism.

For some of us, this might be the scariest idea ever

because you are horrified at letting anyone see the real you. You have hidden behind a variety of identities and accomplishments that define you … but none of those are the real you. For others, you may go to the other end of this spectrum and throw all your stuff on the table to anyone and everyone. Like so many things in life it is a balance. I'm going to say something crazy here: let your feelings be the guide. Well, specifically two feelings: *relaxed* verses *nervous*. When you're really being you and sharing your whole heart with someone, it's like that feeling when you have to go to the bathroom. Once you finally go … Ahhhh, relaxed. Now, don't get me wrong, when you're putting it all out there or sharing the unspeakable or even dreams, it's very scary. What I want you to pay attention to is how you feel after someone responds to whatever you just said.

Being authentic in your daily walk is really hard. A lot of it has to do with boundaries. When you realize that your choices are not confined to "being fake by not sharing" OR "telling it all," you are on the right track. It's okay to give short answers, and it's not being "fake" if you don't give all the information. For example, someone asks you the dreaded, "How are you?" question (gulp); you don't have to tell them all the reasons you're walking through a freaking nightmare. A simple, "I've been better" is totally sufficient for the grocery clerk. Or even when the well-meaning friend from church asks, "How are things going with your divorce?", you don't have to give her the play-by-play.

A simple, "Meh, it sucks but I don't really want to talk about it" is totally fine. *Save the details for your people.* Some have just one person, some have several, some have a dozen. There's no right amount of "your people" just recognize healthy relationships take time.

A word of warning when you're new to boundary setting: you will feel mean and people will call you mean, especially your ex. Setting boundaries can be so uncomfortable as you sit in the statement of what you just told them not being okay with you. *It is so much easier to go with the flow but likely some variation of that is what got you here today.* Ouch! I say that not to be mean, but because I want you to realize the significance of boundaries.

Just to further confuse you, boundaries or at least the word/concept are often misused — I'll gracefully insert the word — *unintentionally.* If you're feeling like you are not sure about this whole boundary concept and it's all new to you, Dr. Henry Cloud and Dr. John Townsend wrote a classic counseling book called *Boundaries.* There are lots of wonderful resources on the internet to help you better understand and practice this task. Sometimes we can understand the concept but are not quite able to connect the dots. I want this book to be a very practical guide, and part of that is keeping it somewhat concise. But when you want more information on a subject, I want to point you to good sources to further your understanding. On my website you can create a free account to unlock many more free resources such as a list of other books I recommend on various topics I lightly touch on.

Back to your heart: maybe you're from a family where the men have left their wives for generations. What do you wish someone would have told you as a child? What have you learned so far that can change the path for your children if you teach it to them? What if you teach them boundaries? What does that look like and how different would have it been for you if you had some boundaries in your teenage years?

Please take a moment and write a little somewhere else. Your prompt: What would I tell my teenage self that would have changed the course of my life? Introspection is an important step in the transition from surviving to thriving. We must analyze our past behaviors to improve the future version of us.

9

LONELINESS

I LOVE THIS QUOTE by Lysa TerKeurst, "Grieving is dreaming in reverse." Both dreaming and grieving are focused on the future. With dreaming, we speak of all the things we hope will happen. *With grieving, we have to find a way to let go of all the things that won't happen*. It so eloquently describes the process of letting go in an authentic way when the vision of our future is shattered. My heart breaks for the millions of people around the world that will experience this pain.

One of the biggest adjustments post-divorce was learning to live alone again. I mean yes, I had two children in the home the majority of the time, BUT I still felt very alone. It was weird and awful. No matter how bad things were in my marriage, it was hard to be alone. Now there were some wonderful things that were mentioned in Chapter 5 as I rediscovered how I liked to spend my time in the evenings, but it was still incredibly hard, even to the day I re-married. I know that's not the case for everyone and many women adjust to this better than my experience. It could have to do with the fact that I'm an extrovert, so I just really like to be around people in general.

Sorry to drop that bomb on you; I love to give hope but I know that is a harsh reality to face. I can try to sugar-coat it with all the positives, but I also think it's important not to downplay how truly hard the loneliness is. I want to validate your feelings — it is hard. It goes back to that Chapter 2 analogy of our identity being shattered. Who are you without your plus one? When you're used to having someone to talk to at the end of your day or the end of your night, it doesn't matter what a jerk that person was, *you were used to them.* You are sitting in something you are not used to; you will get more used to it or you may just realize ways to cope. *When we can recognize it as hard, we can also recognize we will need tools to get through it.*

When I talk about getting through, there is an underlying message of "we get through because we have to." Do you have to? I'm going to boldly call out the real struggle for some going through divorce: the desire to give up on living, because to keep walking is incredibly devastating. If this is where you're at, take a moment and program the Suicide Prevention Hotline into your phone: 1-800-273-8255. Don't be afraid to call if these thoughts begin to overtake you — you are not alone. For many, it's just a passing thought, but for others lingers a little more than they'd like to admit. It's okay to face that reality. The worst thing you can do is tamp it down. Don't be afraid to reach out when you need more help than your best friend can provide. Often clinical depression is like quicksand: the longer you stand in it and the more you struggle by yourself, the harder it is to get out. Working with a trained professional before you're neck deep is ideal; it won't get as scary and will take less effort to get out if you seek help sooner rather than later.

Interestingly, when you look at the research surrounding loneliness, it is very hard to study because loneliness is a relative term – meaning it only exists as you define it for yourself. That simply not spending much time with people doesn't mean you're lonely. On the contrary, as I pointed out at the beginning of this chapter, I felt very alone even though I was around other little people in my life. That loneliness came from being used to something else.

While I would like to say, just "redefine your loneliness," I don't think that's a reasonable encouragement. Though I do think it's worthwhile to self-reflect on what specifically you are missing and get creative in meeting that need. Here's the thing: it's a *need* not a *want*. That need looks a million different ways for different people.

For me, I love being asked, "How was your day?" If I'm honest, this didn't even necessarily happen most days when I was married, but to me the essence of this question was verbally processing life. Now, do I need a boyfriend to meet this need? Nope! Not even a male. What I realized was that I could reach out to one of my other newly divorced friends who was feeling this same hole in her life and we could mutually connect either over text or phone after our kids went to sleep. It was a beautiful arrangement. She also helped me to normalize a lot of the feelings and thoughts I thought I was alone in because she was having them, too.

Another area I struggled to figure out without a husband around was large social situations. You see, I'm sort of a one or two best friend type of person. While I may talk to a lot of people at a large gathering, I really like to return to my person and give them the rundown on everything I learned, and it helps me to remember details in the future. Now that I didn't have my person, I felt off-kilter. I realized that just because I had a habit of verbally processing, it didn't mean I needed to continue to do it that way. I learned to do one of two things: journal it or just think about it. I came to recognize that it's different now, and that's okay.

One alternative if you really need to verbally process: call your best friend. I was leery of that path though because all my best friends are married and I didn't want to tread on their time with their spouse or have them feel like they needed to specifically fill this gap. I encourage you to be mindful in the same way as you overcome your loneliness; sometimes we must figure out what gaps just can't be filled right now and what we can do instead.

Sometimes this can be a spiritual answer. For me, sitting in my loneliness and all the "what the heck has happened to my life?" or "this was not my plan!" was the crying out of my heart in prayer to my Creator. I had to realize that part of acceptance for this stage of life was allowing myself to hate that my marriage ended in divorce. I wanted to be a "success story," where all of a sudden a spouse became remorseful and changed their ways. But the reality was, that wasn't my story. I refused to get stuck. I refuse to be the victim of my story. I used that to propel me towards change, to motivate me to figure out where my marriage got off track. What did I need to do different to set boundaries to protect me from this happening again? Not only to me but so that I didn't teach my girls to let a man treat her badly and justify it to herself as okay. Eventually it motivated me to consider dating again, more on that in Chapter 16. Remember, you got to get "you" right first!

Maybe it's meditation. Slow deep breathing does the soul good. Breathing in five counts, "I'm here for a reason." Breathing out seven counts, "Loneliness is not for me." Whatever it is, you need to breathe in more positive and out more negative. *You will find acceptance of yourself if you seek it.*

What if you shifted your way of thinking of this phase of life not as negative but as *different*? I encourage you to take on the mentality that this new chapter of life is not only full of everything that went wrong leading to a dead end, but instead this new chapter is when everything started to go right. This is when you finally became YOU: the person you were meant to be. Truly think, if it were not for all the negative emotions and experiences you are suffering through, then you would have never become the person you are blooming into. Maybe that person you are just catching glimpses of; she is there, take hope! Keep digging.

I love to travel; not long far away adventures but just a change of environment and exploring new things. It's also something I had to rethink post-divorce. Maybe I didn't have as much money, but I also had the freedom to take little kid-free weekend trips once my kids started spending the night at their dad's. It was fun to plan road trips largely focused on what sounded exciting to us and fit with my work schedule. No longer having to consider my husband's needs or wants was a huge freedom!

The first big trip I did with my kids was a four-state road trip in only one week! I was worried; can I do all that driving? Is it safe for me to do without another adult? Will it be fun? Will I be totally exhausted with no help? Guys, it was one of my favorite trips of all time and my kids were troopers! It made me so excited for the future. I realized that with my ex in the past was a real drag, envision a giant, grumpy toddler. In this new form of vacationing, even when we got lost, we made a random stop that was so fun. We made lemonade out of lemons. I learned to go to bed shortly after them so we could all be on the same sleep schedule. Overall, we just enjoyed every moment and laughed a lot. For example, I planned to have us do a little hike when we arrived at Zion National Park but didn't realize that just because there are pine trees in the pictures doesn't mean there would be cool weather. It was over one hundred degrees when we arrived! A half mile in, we decided we could see the sights just fine floating around like crocodiles in the icy cold stream running parallel to the trail.

The point is my attitude, flexibility, and humor made all the difference. We were used to something completely different that I thought would be missed, but then we realized "different" wasn't necessarily "worse." In fact, it was quite possibly much better! In Psychology, there's a whole counseling approach called Cognitive Behavioral Therapy (CBT) focused on changing your thinking in order to change your behavior. What perceptions or truth do you hold on to that may no longer be true? Maybe it's your style that no longer fits you. What box did you let your spouse or maybe even your family of origin put you in? It's time for you to redefine who you are — you get to decide who that is. Maybe you have always wanted to be more adventurous and do more spontaneous things, but your ex-spouse held you back ... well, no time like the present! Figure it out and live that life.

What other areas do you feel the loneliness? Where

do you need to change your thinking to embrace the mentality of *not wrong, just different*. What things can you change with actions to lessen the feelings of loneliness? What areas can you really only change your attitude?

I can't stress enough: seek out other people going through divorce. There are so many threads of similarity that you will connect on that people outside of this struggle just won't. Not only will they get it, but you can also brainstorm different solutions together. Even just hearing how they are handling common struggles, whether it be emotional or logistical, will help tremendously.

I'm all about setting goals. And guess who I'm most competitive with? Myself! Judge away, I know I'm a nerd — I've embraced that as part of my identity. Now that we've established that, I want to encourage you to set a goal to propel you away from loneliness. Here are some very practical ideas for your goal. Pick the one that excites you most.

1. Join a DivorceCare group.
2. Text friends or post on Facebook asking your friends if they're willing to connect you to a friend that's going through divorce, too and have coffee with that person. (*Friend must be the same sex as you; no dating yet or even thinking about it.*)
3. Join a Bible study.
4. Join a sports team in the city you live in.

5. Join a book club.
6. Join a Google Meet-up group of something you enjoy ... there's one for everything! I joined one for people in my age bracket that meet up monthly to play socially deceptive board games; a super random group of people and really surprisingly fun.
7. Reconnect with an old friend from high school you lost touch with in the chaos of life.

Okay, got it? Not sure? Stop reading and pick one — seriously don't read on. Okay, now write it on a notecard or a post-it and put it on your bathroom mirror until you accomplish it. If you don't want to be lonely, do something about it. Realize that you make choices, constantly, and those choices have consequences. Let these be positive choices that lead you on the path towards the person you want to be.

Speaking of the person you want to be, can we talk vision boards for a second? Okay, put aside all you know about them or any preconceived notions you have around them as cheesy hokey garbage. They are seriously POWERFUL! While I once stood in the camp of making fun of people who did them for longer than I would like to admit, one day I decided to create my own after giving a friend a hard time for saying he needed one. Go figure! Lo and behold, that little piece of garbage changed my life!

While I strongly encourage my clients not to over-think the process, I do think there's a wrong way to make them. What you don't want to do is go in with a preconceived picture of what you're looking to put on your board. You don't want to complicate it; just let it flow. Here's what I encourage you to do:

1. Pick up at least one canvas (I encourage you to split a pack with a few friends) about 12x18 inch or slightly larger size. There's a happy medium of not too big, not too small.

2. Next, everyone Bring Your Own Magazines (BYOM). It is good to have about five from a variety of categories of interest to you. *Hint: Old magazines can usually be bought for less than a dollar at your local library.*

3. Everyone needs their own scissors, sponge paint brush and some Mod Podge. All items can be purchased on Amazon, Target or any local craft store.

4. Optional: Wine and music you like.

5. Start cutting! What pictures/sayings/words jump out at you? Don't overthink it! Just because you cut it out doesn't mean you have to use it. Don't cut out stuff for your friends, focus on YOU.

6. Start arranging what you cut out. Some people do this as they go and some do it all at the end. There's not a wrong way to do

this part. Some people overlap them, and some people space them out. What is visually pleasing to you? Do that.

7. Mod Podge it all down, and hang it up somewhere you will have a few moments to privately reflect on it every day! I like the bathroom, personally.

I swear to you, you will not believe the power of this activity. This is a visual representation of your hopes and dreams. What I have seen time and time again is how mine becomes truth in a way I maybe didn't even understand when I glued it down. Admittedly, there is a bit of a psychic element at play, like where you bring meaning to pictures based on your experiences and link things. The point is, you have a vision, and you are striving after it. Life is no longer passively happening to you; you are chasing after it and defining it for yourself.

At some point, if you haven't yet, figure out who you want to listen to in your life. Who encourages you? Who allows you to dream? Who do you hesitate to share your dreams with? Who do you say the unthinkable to and they just hold your secrets? Who reminds you what got you through the last hard time? If you have no one in your life for the positive questions here, you need new friends. Maybe there's even a cousin or aunt that you haven't been that close to but now's a good time to get to know them more. It doesn't matter where you find these people just that you find them. Just like you need to be doing activities that fill you up, you also need people that pour into you.

There's no shame in admitting that you are lonely. If middle school voices start speaking into your insecurities, use your adult self to tell them, "silence, fools!" Your mind has so much to process right now; I encourage you not to fill up the silence simply because it's painful. The pain is part of the process towards thriving; it sucks, but it is so worth it for "future you." You will get through this.

10

ARE YOU ENOUGH?

Please don't skip this chapter! We have talked about re-discovering yourself, loneliness, and starting to dream and envision a new future, but a lot of times *we are our own worst enemy*. We get tangled up in all our childhood crap, all we haven't done, everything we're not … How dare you change? Who do you think you are to become a better rendition of yourself right now? Maybe these are some of the internal questions you feel looming. Is anyone saying it? Sometimes it's internal, sometimes the person who beat us down in our childhood lives on in our head or maybe they're right upstairs actually saying those things. To that I say: only you get to decide who counts. Stop blaming other people. If you're going to do it different you absolutely must look in the mirror.

There are so many ways we can try to prove we are good enough to everyone around us. If that's your goal, you will never achieve it. I have worked with and have been friends with many highly accomplished people and will tell you that many of them couldn't possibly achieve more to prove this. They are sadly left hanging with, "If I just _____ then _____ ." Nope, you've missed the mark.

When you wrap your identity around your achievements, you will always fall short. However, if you can truly grasp that your worth comes from your purpose, then you will find true joy. The joy that doesn't come from momentary happiness. The joy that continues even on bad days. Here's the crazy thing: you don't even have to define specifically what your purpose is! What?! You just need to have confidence that you are perfectly designed for your purpose in this perfectly orchestrated universe. That if you were done with your purpose, you wouldn't be here. But here you are — so get busy figuring out how somehow all your pain is going to make sense in the big picture! You didn't come this far to get stuck! Your purpose will propel you towards thriving.

I will say, if you have some sense of what your purpose is, kudos! You're lucky because you don't have to deal with the anxiety of not knowing or understanding. I have spent so much of my life trying to figure out my purpose; I've prayed and prayed, switched careers a few times and my undergrad major five times! Here's what I know now: it's not about this moment. It's about being on a path focused on embracing who I am and where I'm able to utilize my gifts. Sometimes it's in small daily conversations, other times it's big things like writing a book! I'm fully writing this book because I feel called to, just stepping into that in obedience — I have no idea what's next! It's one step at a time, focused.

I don't believe in mistakes. Without the hard things, the bends in our path — the unanticipated — we would not have to grow or find alternative paths. If you hadn't gotten fired in 2016, then you may have never left your comfortable salary to start your own business. Often, we're forced into an alternative that was not our desire. When we can embrace the alternative as a necessary part of our story, then we may realize it's function, that it was actually meant to be there all along ... even if it absolutely beyond sucks when you are in it.

If you're like me though, you can embrace it but you don't like it. Guys, I'll be honest, I want so badly to be in control of the universe as it pertains to me. I joke with my husband, "If I was Eve, I would definitely eat the fruit because I want to know all the things and all the answers." The not knowing used to cause me so much anxiety and frustration. But for me, here's the blessing of divorce (haha yeah I obnoxiously just called it a blessing — one I never wanted): when my world unraveled and as I walked through the rubble of post-divorce fallout, I stumbled through it realizing that any semblance of control I thought I had over my life or the people around me was absolutely false. Trying to control people is a false sense of security. They may merely be complying with your wishes to your face, but make no mistake, you never had any control over anyone in any kind of real way. As if the COVID-19 pandemic didn't make it clear, we are only in control of our own actions, not a thing more. We can have the best plan perfectly thought out and — boom, something happens that completely destroys our "perfect plan."

Let your goal be to lean into faith, a power greater than you, verses you trying to control all the outcomes. If we look at it like a continuum from "I control the world" on one side to "God controls the universe" on the other side, I believe you will find sanity right in the middle. But if you want to move beyond sanity, you can lean into your faith to find a peace that surpasses all understanding. On the flip side, when you try to control all the outcomes you may find yourself losing your sanity with situational (not biological) anxiety. How would you like to walk through hell with an inner peace that cannot be rocked no matter what? I'm here to tell you it is possible, I swear.

In the Bible, it's referred to as "a peace that surpasses all understanding." Disclaimer, all I know is my own story, so I have to give credit where credit is due. For me, this true peace came from not only releasing but also accepting that I am not in control, thank God. Literally, I thank God! Because what I realized was that so many pieces of my divorce story were in play for years and years before. For example, being married to someone who continually practiced destructive behavior combined with desperately trying to *make* our marriage work, I had a series of written contracts with my ex-husband of the behaviors he promised not to do anymore, dated with both of our signatures ... like a whole file of them. When I did it, my intention was just to have a written record for us, to memorialize the agreement because what I learned several years into marriage was that I "seemed to remember the conversation differently" than he did. Well, guess what? Now I had a whole file of signed statements showing years of destructive behavior to the court. My ex-husband had me really questioning my perception of reality; gaslighting is the official term for it. I started taking notes because "I never remember things right," and again it worked out very well in court. Once I was out of the marriage, these notes gave me the certainty I needed and reminded me that divorce was my best option. I hated it though. Divorce really wasn't a decision I ever wanted to face.

In a different way, as I touched on earlier, the financial provision in my story came in a way that was so far beyond my wildest dreams. It was almost forty years in the making! If I had received this huge chunk of inheritance a year earlier, it would likely be half his! Instead, I got to finish my professional licensing process and buy my dream car (you're probably going to laugh, it's a white Toyota 4Runner). This as a stand-alone event may sound just like luck, but guys, it was this, fifty different ways. Too much coincidence to be luck. It was me wanting to move and put my kids on a dream charter school waitlist; I only hoped sometime that year one of them might get in so the other could start the following school year … yet they both got into that school within a couple weeks of each other the month I moved to the area. That — over and over again.

When I let go and stopped trying to make things happen, I was in awe of how things fell into place. Now, I'm not saying don't do anything. Let me be super clear: you still must do the footwork. Growing up in the church, sometimes I observed people who took "allowing God to guide their steps" as I'm-gonna-just-sit-on-the-sidelines-and-do-nothing. Do something — anything — literally even if it's just to see if that door closes. Often there are many paths to our destination, but you will never get to the destination if you don't pick a path to start walking.

Okay, so that was a lot of path metaphors! Let's get really practical in what this looks like. Say you know you need to move out of your current house. On the front end this can feel VERY overwhelming now more than ever; you likely don't have a partner helping you with the packing and the physical lifting of things, and then there's also all the emotions of leaving the memories — good and bad — in that house. Then you must pick, all by yourself, where you're going to go. Maybe you're picking by yourself for the first time ever; that can be wonderful AND crazy overwhelming at the same time.

Break the decision down in steps. I'm a big fan of written lists; I reflect so much better when I see it visually. I really love to brainstorm on whiteboards. Consider a bubble chart. Do you remember those? Put the thing you're trying to figure out in a cloud in the middle — so in this example you'd write the word "home." Now draw lines coming out of your cloud with the things you want/need to meet your next home criteria. For example: price range, number of bedrooms, close to your kid's school, attached garage, laundry room... you name it, whatever is important to you. For me, I realized since it was just me now and we spent a majority of our time away from home, I wanted something under a certain square footage as part of a simpler lifestyle. You see, on my vision board was traveling more, wandering, creating, doing life with other people, developing my career and all of these things meant being away from home more.

This idea of making your vision into reality is easy for some and hard for others, neither is better, just different. If it's hard for you, it probably means you're good at enjoying the moment and being fully present. If it's easy for you, it probably means what I just said can be a struggle because you are better at seeing the big picture. In reality it may be harder now for many simply because the higher-than-normal amount of stress you are under. So, make your bubble chart to help you with decision making so you don't get stuck every time you need to decide something. Once we accept that there isn't a wrong path per se, but rather different paths, it takes the pressure of decision making off — that's the goal here.

Maybe a bubble chart doesn't work for the decision you are trying to make. Maybe a good old list of pros and cons will help you sort out your thoughts. Sometimes journaling out the decision can help us realize that we had a preference more than we thought. Or writing about what life would be like in different scenarios you are exploring can really help one to visualize what it would be like. You must figure out which one works well for you and the decision you are trying to make. You might have to try a few, but the point is: I want you to figure it out all by yourself ... because you can and need to build this skill in order to build your self-efficacy. I'm a visual thinker so that's what worked for me.

For me, this process includes praying before, during, or after I'm analyzing some of the written tools above. I pray for guidance; maybe you ask the universe to reveal its will to you. I don't know what's going to work for you, but I want you to recognize that there's something bigger than you controlling the universe. You do you; I only know what worked for me.

My intention isn't to give you all the answers, only to guide (okay, maybe push) you towards a positive destination. When I try to work with clients in private practice on the core issue of "am I enough?", it always comes back to realizing that they are, not because of their experiences or accomplishments but because of who they are. We are actually all born "enough." Our great creator designed us just so, perfectly unique, for our purpose and every life experience culminates into our journey, that somehow some way this all makes sense. Sometimes we hate our journey, to that I say, "use your pain."

I know, I'm the worst! I just told you to use your pain! I'm not trying to glance over it as not relevant, I'm trying to get you to value it. I recognize you have a gaping wound right now, one that is gushing emotional blood that you think may kill you at times. If someone had told me this early on, it honestly would have just pissed me off. I'm pretty sure a few did and I just shook them off in the "you're lucky you don't understand" category. But guys, I have walked this path and I swear to you on everything I have, if you let it, divorce will make you a better person. On the flip side, it can also eat you up and destroy you. You get to choose.

You choose how you're going to respond to divorce; you choose "I am enough." When you stop giving everyone the power to tell you if you're enough and you just decide you are, world watch out! The chains are off and you will walk in freedom to just *be*. Not a perfect person — not even close! When you can sit in your imperfection as okay, every negative part of you has a flip side in the positive you can lean into. For example, critical also means detail-oriented, or rambunctious can also be high-energy. When you truly grasp your likes and dislikes as okay, you can stop trying to be what everyone else thinks you should be or do or say; there is so much self-acceptance and peace.

Let me be clear, the people around you may not love this new you, and know it can be a bit difficult to gently navigate without just coming off as self-focused. The art of figuring out when to compromise and when to gently put forth who you are is challenging. For example, my extended family and many people in the circles I run love to camp. I don't, but I've always fought that because honestly, I love the idea of camping. The reality is, I really like to be clean — and the two do not go together. But for years I have gone on camping trips to appease different people in my life and never even mentioned how much I don't like camping because I just want to have quality time with them. Pay attention: I never even told them I don't like camping. I created my own sense of shame for not being able to simply accept that I don't like camping. I thought if I just kept doing it, maybe I'd start liking it. Now the point isn't that I threw down the gauntlet and refused to never go camping again because I definitely think there's a "worth it" factor where the good outweighs the bad, but the issue was I couldn't even admit to myself that I didn't like camping let alone to anyone else. It may sound silly, but I did this a million different ways and lost my sense of self in the process. *Stop trying to pretend you are someone you're not; it's how you will truly be comfortable and secure in your own skin.*

As mentioned in a different chapter, in light of redefining your new use of time, I mentioned that I love to read but had given that up in the course of my marriage largely to allow my spouse's preferences over my own. Honestly, he didn't do anything wrong in this instance, but I gave him that power. He never asked me to, I just didn't value my preferences or latch on to who I was designed to be.

Another example is biking. I love the idea of it; I did it a lot growing up and my dad's really into it; it's outdoors and active. I really wanted to like biking ... but I don't. And that's okay! It's okay because other people don't shape you, you are already shaped. Does it mean you don't go on the occasional bike ride to appease someone else in your life, maybe or maybe not, you decide if it's worth it. Just be real with yourself. Maybe you even tell the person, "I like spending time with you so much I'll even go on a bike ride for you!" with a wink. Maybe this concept is most obvious when it comes to playing with your kids, especially when they're young. I don't know about you, but I don't love playing Barbies. Does that mean I never play them? No, I will because it's one way I can connect with my daughter on her level. She feels loved and important when I do it. Now do I play Barbies with her every day? Definitely not. The concept is bringing awareness to what you do and do not enjoy doing; sometimes doing the things we do not enjoy still have a "worth it" value that makes them worthwhile.

Maybe you feel like you don't "mom" right … I really struggled here. I know I love working but that is often a point of shame within mom groups or driven hard into me by my own mom. I was raised by a mom that taught: you can't work and be a good mom. I struggled with this "truth" for many years. I really wanted to be a good mom, but if I'm not working, I only feel half alive at best. That's hard for me to sit in, even now. I always wished I was one of those moms who felt full contentment in running a Pinterest-perfect household. The reality is, that's not me. I've joked about starting a blog of Pinterest fails; I love crafts, but they don't love me. I don't love cooking. I love my kiddos to pieces, but I'm a better mom if I'm not with them all the time. If I get time away, I'm intentional about quality time when I am with them rather than just grinding it out unhappily. The reality is that it is not an either/or choice. I don't have to choose between being a good mom OR having a career. That the best version of me actually is a combination — a combination that takes a lot of creativity and problem-solving skills in logistics to make it a reality that works well for me. It also meant that I might have to give up other areas that were less important than holding those two values. For example, I have always struggled to figure out where exercise consistently fits in because I'm not quite as motivated in that area, if I'm being honest.

When I embrace this truth about how I'm wired, I get to shed trying to be someone I'm not, and it helps me to boldly show others that different isn't wrong, it's just different.

A word of caution, when you really embrace who you are, sometimes it makes other people uncomfortable or competitive with you. The sense of security you have may bring out other people's insecurity. They may say mean things, but recognize that people who are hurting often unintentionally hurt other people — think of them as grumpy, wounded animals. The good news is: you tend to attract like-minded people, so stable people tend to attract other stable people. More reasons to wait to date; more on that in the last chapter of this book.

For the most part, how we come to acceptance of ourselves is really an inward process. Yes, it will definitely impact your relationships. It can be challenging for your family of origin to let you out of whatever box you've allowed them to put you in. Just realize, *you allowed them to put you there!* If you want to gently try to break out of that box, try not to attack them; you need people to support you now more than ever. It is okay to speak to them about any specific words that hurt your heart. Trying to prove them wrong is ineffective. Your better option is just to let them know they are hurting you. Be specific, for example: "When you make comments about how clumsy I am, I feel incapable; right now I feel like I'm failing at so many things. If you could just not metaphorically kick me while I'm already down, I'd really appreciate some extra kindness." They might try to justify their words in the moment, but likely they'll be more aware of their words moving forward.

Ultimately, not everyone is kind, and no one is kind all the time. If you want grace from other people, it's important to give it in abundance to others. Part of being enough can sometimes include making amends. Sometimes the choices we make in our marriage (in our desperate attempts to save it) may have caused us to unintentionally hurt other relationships in our lives. While we can't undo those things, we can acknowledge them to the person and wholeheartedly ask for forgiveness. This can certainly be challenging to get out and sometimes doing it in a letter so we get our wording just right is our best option.

Take a moment to think through anyone you might have hurt throughout your marriage. Maybe a wedding you didn't attend because your spouse didn't want to go? A friendship you let go? A family member in another state you haven't visited in years? A parent who tried to speak truth into your life about your spouse when you weren't ready to hear it and you lashed out at them? Old co-workers you continually turned down lunch invitations from because your ex-spouse didn't approve? Think through the different social circles of your life or the ones that faded away; maybe these are regrets. Saying sorry doesn't mean reconciliation, or at least not right away, but it does mean keeping your side of the street clean and hope-fully brings you a sense of closure. If you think it's too far in the past to bring up, I can tell you as a counselor how frequently people are deeply wounded by seem-ingly small things in the past. I can also tell you person-ally how it helped many of my relationships to revisit some of these things.

One example I can think of is when my sister was deeply hurt that I never visited her while her husband was on a very dangerous deployment that was extremely emotionally difficult for their family. Honestly, it looked like a total jerk move from what she knew … but there was a lot more to the story and once I let her in on that it hugely helped our relationship. You see, she also was left to believe my unwillingness to visit her must have been a result of her actions; that she must have done something that really made me mad. In reality it had absolutely nothing to do with her and everything to do with the dysfunction in my marriage. What other relationships in your life need healing?

Okay, now the counselor in me is going to encourage you to do the thing none of us like to do: connect the hang-ups we have now to our past. I love Brené Brown so much and in her TED Talk on vulner-ability, she shares about her breakdown. Specifically, her initial experience with counseling. I can totally relate to "no childhood shit." I hate it; I totally refused to blame my parents. They weren't perfect, but I knew they did better than their parents and they tried really hard. Can I just give them an "A for effort" and leave it there? Nope. It's not about blame, it's about understanding the "why" so we can stop the cycle. We pass our crap onto our kids unless we figure it out. Dang, I know that motivated me!

These are our blind spots. I honestly don't think you can figure this area out by yourself because so often we don't even realize these blundering behaviors are wrong because it's all we know and what is familiar. You can know something is wrong but often not be able to find the root when it comes to your own behavior. Let me make this real in my own story.

One of the hardest generational hurt behaviors that I see unintentionally passed down in my family is criticism. I swear this freaking curse is taught with the best of intention out of love and habit. Along with morals and a strong sense of right and wrong, I was held to an extremely high and unattainable level of perfection. From looks, to grades, to keeping a household: perfection was the expectation. At the ripe age of sixteen, I developed an ulcer trying to please one of my parents, trying to live up to these standards. I mean, they seemed to think their expectations were reasonable — they seemed to be doing it, so should I. Until I realized it was killing me (literally, it felt like it). I realized at sixteen that I could never please this parent and verbally said I would stop trying. I spent another twenty years actually figuring out how to stop letting this person dictate my sense of self-worth. Maybe this sounds crazy, or maybe it sounds familiar. The point was: I couldn't pinpoint the root of so many of my harmful choices by myself. Sometimes we need a counselor, mentor or a wise friend to see the link from afar. I recommend a counselor because I think it's too big of an emotional risk for a friend to speak the hard truth, although occasionally I think it happens because the other person is ready to see it and make changes.

Once you know where these deep roots came from, you get to actively try to bring awareness to your relationships moving forward; whether it's with your kids or future spouse, your goal is to do it different now that you know. I remember my counselor telling me, "You get the love you think you deserve." It took me a long time to agree with her. We actually teach people how to love us in a million small ways.

For example, one of the themes I've had to overcome is that I don't matter. That there is zero weight given to my preference or desire. Now it would be easy to blame my ex-spouse for this, but the reality is, I taught him. I taught him in a million tiny ways. It was modeled to me as a child by a parent. I'm not talking about picking restaurants, although maybe in a tiny way, yes, that's a reflection. I'm talking about "my time does not matter." That everything everyone else needs me to do is more important. I was willing to give up my career so I could run around doing everyone else's miscellaneous stuff. I stopped working out because that ever-growing to-do list was always more important than my health. I made sure my kids made it to the dentist and doctor for excellent care, but I will let my own medical issues go unaddressed for weeks or even months because everyone else's stuff took precedence. Let me tell you, there is never enough time; you have to claim it. Heck if you're like me, you have to battle it constantly as an ever-present default reality.

We do what is familiar; inevitably every family has their things because no family is perfect. It's important to note, in my example above I blame no one. Yes, I learned it from someone, but you know what, I'm almost forty; it's been a long time since I lived under my parent's roof. While it is important to figure out what your family taught you, good and bad, don't start blaming them for your life choices ... they were still *your* life choices.

The first step of Alcoholics Anonymous is admitting that you have a problem. From there, the focus is on changing your behavior to get a more desirable outcome and eventually a better life. I want that for you. It's not easy, though. In fact, I think often when our ex-spouse does "the big things" that are easy to point to for why our marriage ended, it's tempting to put all the blame on them. While yes, that might be the big why, but no marriage is perfect, and I really have no doubt that you played a role in the big thing. Yikes, okay, let me be clear, it's not your fault the big thing happened ... I'm just saying there's a reason you were drawn to that person, there's a reason you tolerated them, there's a reason it's hard to be alone — there was something there. Maybe she reminded you of your mom, both in good ways and some things you swore you'd never tolerate. Maybe he reminded you of your dad, and even though you swore you'd never marry an addict, you somehow didn't see he was one all along. It felt familiar and without awareness you will be drawn to the familiar again.

Perhaps a parent was extremely critical, that they constantly held you to an unachievable high bar. Of course you didn't realize through your adolescent years that your peers weren't being criticized by their parents for everything from the latest pimple that appeared to the one "B" on a report card. Likely it didn't even occur to you to ask them. That's the thing with our family experience, as our norms are developed, they are all we know. Until an age somewhere in the double digits, your brain is literally not even capable of realizing that alternative experiences are even possible.

That's why I want to encourage you to work with a counselor individually. It is so hard to pull ourselves far enough away from our own stuff to see things clearly. It's why as counselors we can guide and point out other people's stuff but it can be so hard to see it in our own life. You just don't know until you know. Think of it like an airplane view: the counselor gets the airplane view and it's very top level. You can't get the airplane view of Earth when you're walking down the street.

If I've convinced you to get counseling, great! I know it can be tricky to find a good-fit counselor; I hear it all the time. I'm going to let you in on an odd truth in the counseling world: what makes a great counselor to one person is horrible for another. I have noticed with my own clients that often the ones that really like me, at some point will tell me that I remind them of one of their parents. At first, I thought it was nothing more than coincidence but having thought about it more through the years, I go back to something a professor said in grad school: "A counselor is often the client's first healthy relationship." I have no science to back this up, but I think people do well with a counselor that resembles the parent they may have a strained relationship with. As a general life principle, I never take advice from people I don't want to be like, at least in the area they are giving advice in. While I wouldn't say counselors give advice, they definitely guide your process and perception. Just something to keep in mind, *Psychology Today* has a great, nationwide search database, too. When you're picking a counselor, I recommend one that has gone through divorce because I think they can understand the many unique factors.However, be leery of the one that talks too much about their own story.

I'm writing this smack dab in the middle of the COVID-19 pandemic and I can't help but hear terms like "now more than ever," or "unprecedented times" or "unlike ever before," with which I absolutely agree.

COVID-19 has definitely rocked life as we know it, but I also know that in your world, divorce can feel very much the same way … only not everyone in the country is experiencing the soul-crushing agony of divorce at the same time. For both, we need community — we need hope. Fortunately, because not everyone is being dragged down by divorce around you, they can help prop you up when it just feels like too much.

You need people. Whether your people pray, or light candles or do yoga to call on their higher power, reach out. One of the biggest blessings early on in my story was how my church community just wrapped around me when I felt like I could barely physically stand from the heartache. I am sad to admit that I did not expect this; I expected the opposite. As luck may have it, within a few weeks of separating from my husband, our church happened to launch a message series on how to walk through hard seasons of life with people. What a serendipitous blessing! What an incredible group of women that prayed over me, helped me with childcare, listened as I tried to make sense of it all and what I should do, sent me encouraging texts. They were just there in all the ways I needed.

The crazy thing was, I never anticipated this group being such a huge support. My own judgmental nature almost made me miss out on this! I love the Bible verse Genesis 50:20, paraphrased: "What the enemy means for evil, God turns to good." This situation was the perfect example of that in my own story. Give people the opportunity to walk in this with you, to make your journey just a little more bearable.

Whatever your hang-ups are, be courageous in figuring them out. When you shy from the truth, from digging down deep to finding the root, you miss out; you miss out on all you could be if you were set free from it. The goal is not perfection, it's awareness.

If you can get past embracing you are enough, just as you are, beware of the next hurdle: Who do you think you are? Likely that's not where you are yet, but if it is, Brené Brown has a great book, *I Thought It Was Just Me (But It Isn't)* with a lot of great research to push you past that.

11

DON'T MAKE THEM PICK

EVERYONE LOSES when kids get put in the middle. Avoid it at all costs! Let it be the first thing you and your ex-spouse can agree on as co-parents. If you are not consciously battling this, then you are doing it — it happens so easy! It can happen in a million little ways and your kids (all kids!) are so sensitive to this; it's like somehow misfiring in the survival area of their brain as essential. As they try to make sense of all the changes around divorce, they are often re-defining who their parents "really" are. Guess what is not helpful? One parent intentionally or unintentionally attacking the character of the other parent. *If you're wondering how you can unintentionally attack someone's character, then know you're probably doing it.*

Here's how it happens: framing stories, small comments, you may think you're even stating facts, sharing details they don't *need* to know, asking their opinion on things. Oh man, I'm definitely guilty on that last one! Divorce is so hard and there are so many big decisions being made. My best mommy heart, often with the very best of intentions, wanted to get my kids input or involve them in the decision process. I now know that stressed them out. I had enough information and I needed to just put on my big girl pants and leave them out of it — to make some big decisions all by myself about what was in their best interest.

To help you understand though, I'll be more specific in where I went wrong. I'm embarrassed to even admit that I was asking my four- and seven-year-olds what kind of custody schedule they wanted. Like, "Do you want to see Dad two days after school for a little while or all day on Saturday?" They were tiny little humans who I studied very closely since birth. I could figure this out on my own. My issue was that I was so overwhelmed that I wanted them to take some of the weight of the decision. Now, in my defense, I really had no awareness I was doing that … but that doesn't make it right or helpful. I should have just considered what I know of them and made the decision all by myself.

Just to further humble myself, I will go ahead and generously say that my kid's father was actually way better at this from day one. I knew it was important, I just didn't really understand how to apply the concept.

He did though, because both of his parents had been through divorce a few times. I imagine he knew the weight and the pain it can cause because he had experienced it firsthand. So, I learned from him and my counselor. I really had to learn a lot because naturally I'm a person who wants things to be fair. I want to justify, and if I'm honest, in my early days of divorce, I tended to overshare. Boundaries look different with kids and part of that is remembering who's the adult and who's the child.

One of the habits I tried to counterbalance this against early on was creating an environment for my kids that "dad" wasn't a bad word. I wanted them to be able to talk about their dad freely, to reminisce on old memories as things came up, to just be able to talk about anything in their life without encountering the hostility that was brewing in me about him. This is a very important foundation to set with them. When you're utilizing your open-ended question asking skills from Chapter 4, they can freely talk about the other parent without worrying about your emotional response at the mention of the other parent's name.

Don't be afraid to say sorry. While doing it all correctly all the time would be awesome, that's not a reasonable expectation of yourself. Think of it like a great opportunity to model a simple apology when you realize you have put them in the middle or made them choose between parents. Be specific and try hard not to justify why you did what you did; just acknowledge that it wasn't right, and you'll continue to try to get it right in the future. *When we model to our kids that perfection isn't the expectation, it makes it easier for them to approach you when they fall short, too.*

Give them the words to let you know when you're putting them in the middle. Let them know that you're new to all this, too, and if they could gently let you know when you are placing them in the middle, you'd really appreciate the feedback. An ongoing conversation I've had with my kids as I still navigate this path is encouraging them to utilize the phrase, "I feel in the middle." It's a flag they can wave at any point in any conversation.

Even still, it can be a struggle to ask questions about how they're doing or what they did this weekend without treading into the other parent's domain. One of the things that helps me stay in my lane is checking my motives. Am I asking to gain information about my kids or to gain information on my ex-spouse? I like to give my kids outs like, "If you don't want to talk about this, that's fine. You can change the subject to something you do what to talk about."

I like making my kids be proactive in the conversation — to teach them that sometimes people may bring up stuff they don't want to talk about and shifting the conversation is often easier than just flat saying or yelling, "I don't want to talk about it!" Also, it achieves my goal in kid conversation to connect with them about what's really going on if they change the subject to something they do want to talk about rather than just ending the conversation. The goal is healthy communication.

Can they overuse this flag? I'm going to land on "no." If you're hearing it a lot, I'd question whether there is a bigger issue at play. In that case, I dig into something like, "It's totally fine if you don't want to talk about it, but can you tell me why?" Depending on the age of your kid, they may or may not be able to verbalize this but it's worth a try. Sometimes it can be the setting or intensity of the conversation. Try having hard conversations while doing something else whether it's playing Legos, drawing, or slime. If the focus is on something else, it makes it a little less intense and the words don't have to flow; they can come more intermittently.

Co-parenting is hard. It takes a lot of maturity to not let the emotions going on between the two of you dictate how you parent your kids together. It looks a million different ways and you have to find your groove. Many parents resort to written communication, at least in the early days, assuming your emotions are running high. There are many benefits to this even if it takes a little longer. While court documents are still in the works, it's ideal to have a written record of some sort of what was agreed upon, even if it starts as verbal conversation but then gets memorialized by one parent and accepted in writing by the other. I'm not talking wet signatures, just email.

A few tips when writing emails to address concerns or issues at hand. First, *start with what the other parent is doing right or sincerely acknowledge the effort they are making.* For example, say you're annoyed with how they tend to be 10-15 minutes late to pick the kids up every visitation. Don't start with laying into them about how much stress this brings you and makes you late to work and blah blah blah … I can almost guarantee you will get a response justifying their actions. Instead, I recommend trying to generously give them the benefit of the doubt. In this example, it would look something like, "I know you are juggling a lot right now, more than ever, and I appreciate that you consistently pick the kids up to spend time with them."

Next, *keep it future focused on the kids.* Future-focused gives the other parent the opportunity to do things different. If you ever want your ex to change, you must be willing to let them out of the box. To keep building on the above scenario and to put in play being future focused on the kids, while the other parent being late may really be messing you up, assume that's not the primary issue. Make it about the kids' sake that he shows up when he says he's going to. For example, you would add, "When you're late, it leads our kids to assume that they are not important or priority enough to be on time for." Depending on where you're at with your ex, I'll let you decide whether to mention why whatever issue at hand is important to you. I will say, if things are not going well, don't bother mentioning it as he may disregard your whole concern as a power move or to be vindictive.

Lastly, *offer alternative solutions.* Think outside the box and be solution focused. Try to come up with a few alternatives that would meet the objective. For example, you could say something like, "Would it work better if I dropped them off and you dropped them off to me at the end?" or "Maybe there's someone else that would enjoy seeing them regularly like your parents that could pick them up and buy you a little time to finish up things at work?" Or depending on how old your kids are and if you're comfortable with it, "If you're late, I probably need to leave the kids home alone so that I'm not late for work." These are all very hypothetical, but I hope they help to understand how to apply these tips.

One pitfall that can quickly take you to crazy town is making the issue at hand about something in the past. When you belittle the other person in order to make your point or establish yourself as right, it's not helpful and quite the contrary. For example, when you bring up how much they suck at connecting with your kid versus proactively encouraging behaviors in the future that would support a better relationship, you get a big difference in outcomes or willingness to do what is in the best interest of the child.

One of the hardest things for me to come to terms

with as I grieved my marriage was that I needed to accept that I was never going to get an apology. He had his truth and justification and I had mine. I had to stop trying to convince him that he was a jerk for what he did and just accept that he was broken. I had to come to terms with the fact that I couldn't fix any part of him and given everything that was thrown at him in his upbringing, he was doing the best he could. When I could generously acknowledge that he was doing his best, even if I thought his best was extremely dysfunctional, it was his best-ish. It was hard to acknowledge that his best effort included choices that were extremely hurtful to me. I could acknowledge that his actions made sense to him, but that I no longer had to accept his unacceptable behavior — and these concepts weren't mutually exclusive. The complicated yet simple answer is grace. In the end, I realized that understanding the psychology of his choices allowed me to understand that he wasn't doing it on purpose to hurt me. I was just collateral damage. This allowed me to have compassion for him.

Generously giving grace will help your co-parenting. When you can assume that your ex-spouse is not trying to be a jerk — sometimes they just are — you are giving them grace. When you can assume neutral intentions, overlooked rather than malicious, you are on the right track. Correlation doesn't necessarily mean causation. By that I mean just because two actions go together doesn't mean there's a driving force, maybe it's just chance and likely, you'll be better off if you can take on that mindset.

I love this list of co-parenting success benchmarks pulled from Ron Deal's book *The Smart Stepfamily*:

- We give our children the freedom to love both parents and believe my child's well-being is directly affected by the quality of relationship I have with their other parent.
- The transition between our homes is smooth and positive.
- We intentionally plan out the details of holidays to minimize stress.
- We make it possible for our children to love and maintain ties with both extended families.
- I think the more functional my relationship is with my ex, the less likely it is that our children will engage in high-risk behaviors.
- We recognize the developmental stages of our children and let them enjoy their childhood.
- We allow and encourage our children to take specific clothing, toys, and electronic devices between their homes.
- We encourage our children to have photos of their other parent in their bedroom.
- We tell our children it is okay to talk about how much they miss the other parent.

- I discuss specific parenting strategies with my ex.
- I do not get upset when our child seeks out the other parent after a game or event.
- We speak highly of the other parent to our children
- We communicate regularly with our co-parent.
- We do not allow or utilize the children as messengers or "go-betweens" on anything.
- We are working with our co-parent and stepparents to raise healthy and well-adjusted children.
- I can see a positive difference in my children as a result of our co-parenting efforts.

Please don't get overwhelmed by this list early on in your divorce; it's not reasonable to expect in the beginning months. It's an adjustment that will take time. Look at it more like a list of goals or a roadmap to successful co-parenting. Consider sharing it with your co-parent as targets you want to strive towards. Maybe figure out the handful you really want to focus on in the next six months, share them with your kids, and if they're over ten years old, encourage them to give you feedback.

For kids, divorce often feels so out of their control. It's really hard to find appropriate ways to give them small bits of control. Feedback is one of those ways.

Teaching them to give gentle feedback focused on positive change ideas is a great tool for them. More on that in the next chapter. In fact I'll be breaking down that awesome list of benchmarks above to explain the "why" behind them.

12

LISTENING TO YOUR KIDS

In the co-parenting benchmarks listed at the end of the last chapter, you can see a theme of neutrality. That in the best interest of your children, you're going to have to divide the relationship you have with the other parent to simply ex-spouse and co-parent. If you could paint it as a picture, it would look like two roads merging. As you mourn the loss of your marriage, look at it as if the other person's role as your spouse has morphed solely into "ex-spouse" and should now be simplified to only "co-parent"; that is the only role that person has in your life. That person was in multiple roles while you were married — now they have one: co-parent.

One of the phrases I use as a guiding light in co-parenting, often even in direct conversation with the other parent is, "best interest of the kids." This is the goal, the ideal — "best interest," but often in the first year of divorce, we did not agree on what was best interest. I took it one rung lower to safety. Safety was and is always my minimum threshold in co-parenting decisions. It's about the only time we ever end up before a judge because sometimes we can't even agree on that.

That's the ground view of co-parenting, now let's look at the airplane view. I don't mean to put additional pressure on you, but *you are walking through what will likely be the most traumatic part of your children's childhood.* I'm sorry if that stings, but I want you to see the significance of your actions. I also personally understand the burden to try to be a good parent when you're parallel walking through what might be your most difficult chapter of life, too. Please remember to give yourself grace, because if you're reading this book, I think it's safe to say you are making an effort.

Take time to recognize the effort you're making. That while I give you all these tips and pointers (of what I learned the hard way), I also recognize the agony of walking through it. I want this book to motivate you, but I also want it to be a very practical guide. Part of being practical is recognizing that no one does it perfectly. *Apologies are important to the process;* grace for yourself is important to the process. We are able to give grace easier when we can wholeheartedly receive it ourselves.

Is it odd to talk about receiving grace in a chapter on parenting? No, it's totally relevant! It's so hard! I think it's the one area that even the best of parents struggle to know the best way to handle situations. In this area in particular, you can have good intentions but still do things that make it emotionally more difficult for your kids. It's one area that is still an on-going struggle for me because co-parenting is for the rest of your life in a million different scenarios. There's no sense of "Oh I got this!" and maybe that's why I like Ron Deal's list of benchmarks in the previous chapter because I needed someone to tell me, "Yes, you're on the right track." I swear, co-parenting is the book no one will write because it's so hard to figure out. That's why I think you should latch on to guiding principles rather than hard rules; use your kids mental health as your report card and give yourself grace.

That's top level, ready for some nitty gritty? In Chapter 4, we talked about asking open-ended questions as essential. I've learned that time spent talking is a better goal than the number of questions asked, or I'll get short answers to get it over with. All my questions are focused on them: who's their best friend, what are they learning about life, one nerdy fact they've learned at school lately that was maybe kind of interesting, what she hopes I make her for dinner soon. Then I love to throw in a silly hypothetical question that she usually rolls her eyes at but actually smiles while answering the question. *The point isn't to solve their problems, it's simply to get out what's going on in their head and heart.*

I'm also super direct with my kids on what my

motives are. I will literally tell them, "Hey, I know I'm no competition to your awesome device, but I love you to pieces and want to know how you're really doing." I don't accept "fine" (I literally say that, too). When I ask them how their day was at school and they say "good," I ask "Oh, what made it good?" Or with girls, their friendships tend to be "complex" and I feel like when I have a good grasp on what their struggles and dynamics are in their friendships then I can support them better as a developing human. I don't take items (i.e. devices) out of their hands, I beg/plead/demand that they set them down; it is important that they do it on their own accord or I guarantee any hope of deep conversation will be stomped on.

For all kids, divorce is a big deal but how it looks varies quite a bit; each child is so unique even in the same family. For my youngest, as she tried to figure out and understand divorce, she asked literally every kid she met if their parents are divorced. It was a little funny (and horrifying), but I also came to understand that she was trying to figure out if it changed her identity. What I think she realized is: you really can't tell by looking at someone if their parents are divorced, and kids have a lot of different parent situations. It led to some really interesting conversations and realizing that families can have a lot of different factors; no one way is right or better, just different. It was a *process* for her to come to that understanding and accept it, though.

If you don't know by now, let me make it super

clear: *you can't control your co-parent's actions.* Let your focus be on supporting your kids, not trying to change your ex-spouse; it's time to give that battle up. Maybe this is a given for you, but it wasn't for me. It's my natural inclination to be a hover/smother parent even though I can completely recognize this as unhealthy. I didn't realize it fully, though, until my marriage ended. Divorce took the buffer out for my kid's perception of their dad. It was a harsh reality to face — I wanted to fix it, but I couldn't. I could only be there for them as the floor dropped out.

I don't think you can over-love your children in that first year of divorce. If they're pushing away, it's not because they don't need you; you just need to figure out what part of what you're doing is too much. Sometimes that takes a therapist for you or more likely for them. Sometimes they can't find the words to say what's in the heart or they're afraid to hurt you more. If you think your kids don't know you're hurting, you're wrong, even if you're not crying in front of them. Sometimes they feel like their emotions are too much to put on you. Again, I'm super direct with my kids in asking them the hard questions, "Hey, you know you can talk to me about anything? Is there anything you're scared to tell me because you're afraid of my response? You don't have to tell me what the thing is, I'm just wondering if it's there?"

We teach our kids how to love and how to be loved. How we show up for them and love on them in actions is an investment in their future relationships. If you're busy all the time and don't take the time to sit with them, just sit fully present, they will perceive they don't really matter that much. In their future relationships they will be drawn to the boyfriend or spouse that holds them at bay, not fully invested in them, because that's what they know – that's what is comfortable to them.

As you form your new version of family, I just want to put that truth on your radar, how you love and engage with your children is highly influential to what they will be attracted to in a future mate. Divorce can be a wonderful reset button if you allow it. It allows you to totally change the way you may have been parented, what you know ... to something you wish you had experienced. Be the parent you wish you had.

As mentioned in Chapter 4, sensory play can be really helpful for dealing with big emotions. Consider creating a sensory corner or box in your house where anyone who's feeling upset can go at any point. This empowers them to do something with all the emotions. Empowering your child to deal with their emotions in a healthy manner is an amazing skill to teach them at any age before they leave the nest. Maybe you guys can even think of a positive name for the corner.

A bean bag or swing with a bin or cubby next to it with items is a great idea. Maybe you do this immediately, or maybe it's part of a gift. How you introduce it will make a big difference on their buy-in for utilizing it moving forward. Depending on your kid, some may enjoy being part of the planning process or have ideas of what to include. I have a particularly crafty child who likes to make things, so it's easy to let her spin off on Pinterest "Sensory DIY." However you go about it, the goal is to create something they will use and hopefully you will, too. Sometimes modeling the behavior we'd like to see is the best way to get them to do it. Scrap the old thinking, "Do as I say, not as I do." Bad news, actions speak so much louder than words. *You are modeling how to deal with big emotions.*

What are your actions telling your kids? If you have a teenager in the household, likely they are telling you. Are you expecting more of them than what you are modeling yourself? Maybe it's time to rethink some expectations. Just because you've done things one way doesn't mean you can't shift now; divorce is the perfect excuse! For example, maybe you've always done their laundry, but you're spread so thin now that you need them to help more. Or maybe it's more mental; maybe "old you" never used to ask for their input on vacations, but now that they're a little older, you let them plan out a vacation. Give them a budget and see what they propose. This can be a great activity to suck up some of their time when they complain about being bored in summer. Empower them to do something about their boredom; teach them that they can be active solution finders! One of the things that is hard as a single parent is running a household by yourself. Figure out what things might be fun and or beneficial for them to help with.

I will say, I love for my kids to plan things. They're so creative and I think it's a good life skill. Whether it's a family night like what games you will play, what movie to watch, if there's a theme, what you will eat, making lists and a timeline. They will suck at it at first, but they will learn the skill and love that they got control over it. Likely you have more than one kid, and what one kid plans the other might not be so enthusiastic about — that's okay — they'll have their turn and the other siblings will be subject to it. If they're talking, they are old enough to do some rendition of this. Even when it's horribly bad, it's still fun. You're making new memories and showing them that just being fully present together is fun. Consider having everyone (including you) put your devices in a closet for a few hours while you do this, it will mean a lot to them.

Inevitably, your child will not want to transition to the other home at some point, whether it's the first post-separation visit, a month in or even a year down the road … it just happens sometimes. For many divorced couples this can become a huge issue if you let it. I would encourage you to have a proactive conversation with your co-parent to preemptively get on the same page in preparation for this inescapable day. Most often it has more to do with disliking changing between households than anything else. Sometimes it's a phase that goes on for several visits or sometimes it's just a one-time thing.

While I am a fan of empowering your child with choices, this is not the time. It is the time to present as a united front with your co-parent and teach that seeing the other parent consistently is important. Visitation is not optional, just like going to school is not optional. While it is okay to engage in the conversation of why they don't want to go, try to avoid allowing them to get deeply emotional and worked up. Try to keep it solution-focused and ask problem-solver questions. For example, "Would bringing your stuffy help? Maybe they miss Daddy since they haven't seen him in a while." Or maybe with an older kid it looks like, "What would you do if you didn't go?" because once they realize you're not going to let them go to Sarah's house if they miss their visit, then they may be a lot more willing to go.

You can encourage proactive conversation with the other parent that is solution focused, too. For example, we realized transitions went a lot better on Saturday mornings then Friday after school. One of my children needed to just chill and have a low key evening with her primary parent after a long week of school. It really had nothing to do with not wanting to see Dad and everything to do with not liking change.

Interestingly, some kids enjoy change while others hate it. The ones that hate it will likely throw up some resistance in various forms as they adjust to living in two households. Often it takes more conversation with that child to process the change in a positive manner.

Little changes can make a big difference for these children. One of the other things we learned from our little change-hater is that whoever picks her up from school better be the one she's spending the afternoon with. Turns out one of her triggers was, she hated it when I picked her up and dropped her off immediately at her dad's house. *It is very easy to think that the resistance is because the child must not want to go to Dad's house or that Dad is doing something wrong, so watch your line of questioning to get to the root issue because so often I've found it really has nothing to do with the other parent.*

Another issue we've run into is if for whatever reason one parent has all the pets. One of the things that helped my kids be far more excited to go to their dad's house was when he got them hamsters. It seems like a small thing, but it made such a difference in how they perceived his house as "home." Again, nothing to do with him, we just had to figure out what was missing.

If your child struggles with transitions, one thing that can help is having a calendar in your main room or their room with their visitation schedule on it. My more chill kid found this helpful even at a very young age. It started with a whiteboard that had the days of the week on it and since she wasn't reading, we put the letter "D" with a heart around it on her visit days. Before she went to bed, we would look at the calendar and she could ask any questions. It was super beneficial to her in the early days for conceptualizing it. If your child is missing the other parent, it's helpful for them to know when the next time they will see them is. Another thing I think can be useful is if it's a longer visit (like for the weekend), if the parent's house they are going to be going to gives them some idea of what the plan is for the weekend. They feel much better about going ... even if it's just a few very normal details like, "Saturday we're going to clean a little, go to Target and eat BBQ chicken for dinner." Sounds easy enough, right? Give it a try, then ask your kids if they find it helpful to know or if they don't really care.

Another thing is getting your kids in proximity to the other parent's home; this is especially valuable for younger kids. If you drive to the other parents block and then take a quick little walk around the block before walking up to the house it can help smooth the transition. On that little walk, it's very important to be off your phone and open for listening. Sometimes silence is fine and good, depending on the kid. Some kids like open-ended questions like: "What are you looking forward to on this visit?" or "What's one thing you're excited to tell Dad?" Keep the conversation positive and try to seem excited for them.

What if your child is really missing the other parent? First, legitimize the feelings as okay and recognize that it's a hard situation. Maybe remind them of another change they went through that was really hard at first. For some, it was the first day of preschool or kindergarten. For others, maybe a time they moved.

Help them see that it's okay to feel sad, and then move on to trying to think of ideas that might help. One of the most helpful tools is allowing and encouraging the child to call/text the other parent whenever they are missing them. This isn't always feasible, so an alternative is to write them a note or draw a picture to give to them next time they see them. Another idea is having a special item or stuffy from the parent they are not with at the current parent's house. Example, Dad gives daughter a locket to wear when she's at Mom's house. Sometimes parents prefer a daily set phone call time to ensure regular contact. Some kids get bummed out by that. One of my kids wants no contact with me when she's at her dad's house because it bums her out and then she wants to go home ... but if she doesn't hear from me, she's totally fine.

So, lots of ideas just to further drive home the importance of a positive co-parenting relationship as essential to your child's well-being. You can move forward with confidence knowing that there is a boatload of research to support this notion. The cost of putting your child in the middle and making them choose between parents can be catastrophic; it's hugely linked to drugs, mental health and even suicide. There are so many factors you cannot control that come with co-parenting, and accepting that you can't fix things for your kids is really hard. You can listen to them and oftentimes that makes a huge difference in their experience, just validate that their emotions are real and hard.

While you weren't willing or able to be married to their other parent, this is a gift you can give them that will unquestionably lighten the blow of divorce — the difference between "changing their life" or "ruining their life." You get to choose that ... well most of you do. In the next chapter I'll spend a little time on what I call the outliers. You can read it either to increase your gratitude, or for a little guidance on some of the more uniquely challenging situations that arise from divorce.

13

THE OUTLIERS

UNIQUELY CHALLENGING DIVORCE SITUATIONS

CHOO-CHOO! All aboard the crazy train! I realize that some of you are reading this book thinking your situation is "unique" ... in a bad way. First, I'm sorry — I am really truly deeply sorry that this is the path you are enduring. So many times in my life I have wished I had a magical wand; I would love to make people's problems go away. Gosh dang it, I can't though! This will be the one chapter I'm going to really stay in my therapist role and not go personal. I will say somewhere in here though that I can relate on a few areas and my heart hurts for you. Mel Robbins said, "You have been assigned this mountain so that you can show others it can be moved." That is my journey; I am a living testament that you will survive, and if you allow it, this painful experience will change you to bless others, eventually ... For now, chin up buttercup, you will get through this!

So, you drew the short straw. Divorce is bad enough but you're walking through a freaking horror show. Sound about right? *Here's the real reality: if you were married to someone that falls into one of the categories below, this book is not a complete guide, in fact a lot of the insight either is not applicable or it may even be bad advice.* You're going to need more books and definitely an individual counselor. Wherever your ex-spouse would go to get help (whether they actually do or not) can be a great resource for how you can get help or support. Examples: jail, inpatient mental facility, suicide helpline, domestic violence hotline. Call them! They will be sympathetic, get it and likely want to help you. You won't have to explain, just ask for resources for family members.

Super Sucky Situation #1:
The Jail Bird

Whether you knew what they were up to or not, jail is always a shock when it actually happens. This is a hard topic to write generally about because the situations are so varied. The reality is: you were abandoned one way or another. Likely, you have more anger than your other friends going through divorce. There's no shame in that, but don't let it eat you up. Think of anger like an energy source. Like in a small way, I know that when I'm mad it's a great time to clean ... just imagine what you could do. But think bigger than a clean house — dream big. Despite all the things that have led you down this path, it's not too late for a life change. Think about future you. How do you connect the dots? Make a plan and go for it!

Super Sucky Situation #2:
Gone Without a Trace

The person left, not only you but your kids, and all of the implications and unanswered questions are reeling through your head. You feel rejected. Maybe he said good-bye, or maybe you came home to an empty house. Maybe you know he'll never be back, or maybe you have no idea. Rejection is the theme of your heart issues. This is where you will need to do your hard work. Disclaimer: This is not legal advice … but strongly consider filing for divorce and get all your custody documented through the courts. Many states have a way to serve an individual with legal documents without a known current address. If you don't have money for an attorney, you will want to look on your local family law courthouse website to see if they host free clinics to help you file paperwork. He may change his mind, and you need the abandonment on the record showing instability. Do it for your kids' sake — they need stability now more than ever. Your family likely needs closure, and resources on grief may be very helpful for you and your kids. Even joining a support group for grief could be a good fit; you will likely qualify if you talk to the group leader before attending your first meeting. Writing letters you never send can be helpful; find ways to say all the things you never got to. Find your voice and you will regain your power.

Super Sucky Situation #3:
Domestic Violence

Wounded, maybe it's physically but more likely the greatest pain is from emotional abuse. I will venture to say walking away is the hardest thing you will ever do. It can also be the scariest. I am SO proud of you. Not many people are brave enough to walk away. The same strength that got you away will now be treasured in your heart. You didn't come this far to stop now. I love the term "wounded healer." Unfortunately, domestic violence is way too common; you getting it right will bless and inspire other people. Likely you've already found your "why." Your struggle will be endurance. Your road to change in all areas will be long. Accept the long road knowing that it is worth it. Find ways to stay inspired.

Super Sucky Situation #4:
Pedophilia

I hate that this is a category. I'm so sorry this is your nightmare. Your heart battle will likely be disconnection and shame. It is hard to show up and endure the judgement you will face, even though it had nothing to do with you. Realize and hold that truth close: it had nothing to do with you. I didn't lump it with the other mental illnesses because it is a bit unique. Most people don't understand this. It may help you to educate yourself more on Pedophilia so that you can truly understand how not your fault this path is. A support group will likely be a great resource for you. Keep your kiddos safe; let love and healing flow over your family as they heal. Art is a great outlet for kids/teens.

Super Sucky Situation #5:
Personality Disorders

Did you know that most insurance companies will not cover treatment for personality disorders when it's the primary diagnosis? There are five axes in the Diagnostic and Statistical Manual of Mental Disorders (DSM-IV), and personality disorders are given their very own axis while every single other mental disorder is on another axis! They're called Personality Disorders because they are intrinsic to who that person is ...

so to expect them to "get better" is rarely reasonable. Your heart struggle will likely be creating a sense of self-worth. Often, personality disorders lead a spouse to believe they're someone they're not in reality. If this sounds familiar or you're confused, look up the term "gas-lighting." A word of caution: DO YOUR WORK or you will marry someone else with the same or similar personality disorder. Likely one of your parents had some rendition of one, or strong traits that normalized your experience to crazy town. I'm not blaming you, and I'm really glad you got away from that toxicity. Now you get to grow into the person you were meant to be.

Super Sucky Situation #6:
Major Mental Health Issues

This can look a lot of different ways and be very difficult to walk away from. The guilt you feel from other people who don't understand may be overwhelming at times. Mental illness does not justify the other person's behavior; you are still a person who gets to make choices, too. You might be one of the people who feels like a weight has been lifted when you get out of your marriage — possibly a burden that started so slowly you didn't even notice it crushing you ... until you weren't really living anymore. Your struggle may be custody and safety. You leaving could likely be a sign of your mental wellness. Don't let yourself completely off the hook if when you married the person you kind of knew about the track they were on. There was a reason you were attracted to them; do your counseling work there so you don't fall into a different variation of the same trap.

Super Sucky Situation #7:
Addiction

Let the truth set you free ... if only it was that simple! If you were married to an addict, you likely have, at some level, trust damage. My dad, a recovering alcoholic, used to have a little riddle from AA that may resonate with you: "How do you know when an addict is lying? Their lips are moving!" One of the pitfalls of addiction is the amount of lying required to maintain the front that they're okay. There's tons of great information and resources to understand addiction more. Personally, I love Alcoholics Anonymous (AA), and their co-part Al-Anon is a great support group for people affected by an addict. It's a great place to help you figure out your own role. Because guess what? We get the love we think we deserve ... Yikes, newsflash: addicts don't love well when they're too wrapped up in their own addiction. If you want to ever get married again or run some damage control on your kids, you're going to have to get to the root of how you got here so that history won't repeat itself. Betty Ford (the Gold Standard of recovery centers, in my opinion) partnered with Hazelden to produce some incredible research in this ever-evolving field, but start with AA.

Kid Tip: When it comes to explaining a lot of the above situations to your kids, stick with the phrase, "I don't have words now to help you understand what Dad/Mom went/is going through, but one day I will help you understand better." Focus on their emotions, healthy coping skills, and answering their logistical questions. If your child is over twelve years old they may find an Ala-teen support group helpful.

Whatever your situation is, it will be easy for you to fall into a serious pity party for years or even the rest of your life. You can let divorce ruin you and turn your heart bitter and hostile. That's not really living though; it's just very slowly dying. You get to make the choice. You can absolutely stay stuck. Your friends and family will honestly probably understand because it's more than a lot, what you've been through. I hope and pray that is not the path you choose though.

I would like to suggest that if one day (at least a year after your divorce finalizes) you think about dating and your ex-spouse fell into one of the above categories, put that thing on your deal-breaker list. No matter how awesome the person may seem or if they got counseling or went to rehab, you just don't know and it's absolutely positively not worth that risk to go down the same path. You know what the definition of insanity is? Doing the same dumb thing over and over again and expecting different results.

Let's talk about the "At Least …. " Game. If you have sick humor like me or maybe just trying to survive what has become of your life, when you have no more tears to cry, find a friend (maybe if you're really lucky, one who is enduring some twisted stuff like you) and take solace in the "At Least" Game. My friend and I created this lovely game for when it was just too much; when we'd said "I'm sorry" or "wow, that really blows" way too many times in the conversation, we'd resort to the most obnoxious things we could think of to say to the other person that began with the sentence stem "At least." For example, when your friend is devastated that her ex-husband went out last night with your child's teacher … you say something like, "At least you know she's good with your kid!" Your goal is to set a super low bar and say the most insensitive thing possible that makes the crappy thing seem somehow okay. Now it may not sound that fun but here's what you'll realize, people actually say these things to you! Bless them; they can have the best of intentions … they just have no idea what it's like to walk in your shoes and they're trying to pull in some positivity. Respect that their heart is pure. I'm sure if you're resonating with this chapter, you've mastered the fake smile and nod. Honestly, if this is your path, you don't need to correct them; you've got enough brewing and need all the people on your team you can get. Recognize that their intent is good.

The reality is, you need someone that gets it — even if it's just one person in your life that you can say the unthinkable to. You need someone who gets it, and when it just gets to be too much, you can laugh with. Find a way to find humor. Laugh about the things you used to tell yourself or tried to believe. One of my personal favorite things I used to tell myself: my ex-husband went to raves "for the music" … as a man with children and well into his thirties. My lovely friend mentioned above had a good laugh sarcastically responding, "and mine went to sex parties 'for the snacks.'" Oh man, if we can't laugh at ourselves, we'll never make it. Don't let that person steal your life or your joy; this is a season that will pass. Rise up. *Just because this is where you are right now in life doesn't mean that's where you have to stay.*

14

THE "D" IS DONE, NOW WHAT?

THE DAY HAS COME or nearly come, and your divorce is final. Likely you have all the emotions. One time I asked my now husband what he was feeling before a particularly emotional court hearing and he responded "everything." It was simple and profound. Such a fitting way to describe the barrage of feelings encompassing this milestone.

If you are preparing for this day, please don't make the mistake of thinking this is going to be just like any other day. Because you don't have to go to court (at least not in California) the day your divorce is final, it's easy to think that day will just come and go. Ummm, if you're like me and others I've met ... this day will not go unnoticed. It will probably even feel extra-long. Even if you think it seems like an eternity since you separated, this will still be a big day. I want you to take a moment to think about what the emotions are for you.

Are you happy it's here? Relieved? Sad? Angry? Frustrated? Scared? Exhausted? There is no one way you *should* feel, just be authentic with yourself in what you actually feel.

Consider what you want to do to acknowledge that this day is arriving. I would strongly suggest planning to have a friend accompany you that day at the bare minimum; let them know the significance of the day and that you need them by your side. Like, brace for impact! Maybe you want a whole bunch of friends by your side to celebrate like in the Netflix show "Girlfriend's Guide to Divorce." Maybe you want to burn your wedding dress. Maybe you want to grab dinner with a friend and make a toast to your future. Maybe you want to do a photo shoot trashing your wedding dress. There are lots of great ideas on Pinterest. Figure it out in advance. But please do yourself a favor and don't plan to be alone or think it will be an insignificant day.

> **Kid Tip:** Don't include them in the festivities. They don't need to know the divorce is final; it was over for them when you stopped living in the same house. In general, they should be completely unaware of any of the legal proceedings. That's a parent thing.

You may eventually find yourself feeling ambivalent to your ex-spouse. Do you know what the opposite of love is? It's not hate, but ambivalence. This is when that person just doesn't affect you in the same way anymore. When you stop allowing them to get under your skin in an authentic way. What I mean is when they pull their same old antics, you respond differently. For example, remember when you used to give him a bunch of options of when he could see the kids and it was debilitating for you to plan anything? (I know I'm not alone in trying to push the relationship between the other parent and kids.) Well now, new you just plans activities. You've come to realize the longer he waits to make a decision, he is making his decision to disengage … and that's not your fault. Life carries on, you lay the course.

Now in this example, if you have a custody schedule then absolutely leave those windows open whether he shows up or not. I'm talking about for the co-parent who calls last minute and wants to pick the kids up for dinner. It's okay to hold to whatever you have planned even if it's spaghetti night at home. The point is: you have plans. Now, if making the spaghetti tomorrow night works and a few hours alone sounds good, then yeah, absolutely say yes. But realize that you count. Realize that your kids' plans count, too. If they made plans to go to a friend's house, don't make them cancel last minute because their dad calls last minute and wants to see them. You don't have to be a jerk about it; in fact, I encourage you to gently let the other parent know that you would really like to support the relationship and encourage them to pick a consistent day or pattern for visitation that works for all of you so you can all make sure to plan accordingly. It will benefit everyone involved. All of this is new; you are all learning. Make your motives clear to the other parent so your actions are not misperceived. You can literally say, "I'm not trying to be a jerk. I want you to see the kids regularly, but we just need to be able to plan for it."

What if you don't want the other parent to see the kids? Whew, this is a hard one and I hate to admit I struggled through this at one point. If there have been a lot of lies or poor choices in the marriage, sometimes it can feel like it's not in the kids' best interest to stay in relationship with the other parent. I am here to say that based on the immense quantity of long-term research, there are very few cases that it's not in their best interest. It's why they often let kids visit their parents in jail even! It's why supervised visitation is a thing. If your concerns are legitimate, you probably need to bring it before a judge or make a Child Protective Services (CPS) report and let them determine how best to keep your child safe while remaining in some form of contact with the other parent. I know it's horrifying, but I swear to you: the long-term effects of that parent abandonment are HUGE! I'm talking major correlations in addiction, suicidal ideation, dysfunctional relationships, abuse — basically all the things you have nightmares about for your kids' futures. And let me tell you, your

kids will one day be angry at you if did it out of court.
Let the court take the hit. All you have to do is let them
know what your concerns are and why you think that
(a.k.a. proof if you have it).

> **Co-Parenting Tip:** One of the ways I communi-
> cate with my children's father over concerns is
> utilizing *two baselines: best interest of the kids and
> safety.* Best interest is the ideal, like when I'm
> trying to explain why I don't think something is
> good for them in some way. Honestly, we often
> don't agree here and while it sucks, that's okay.
> The reality is that even in marriage parents
> often don't agree on best interest. Where I will
> seek legal recourse is if I have a major safety
> concern. I'm not talking a broken bone; I'm
> talking about dying. I literally have to think,
> will this action kill them? The gray area here is
> kidnapping; while the action will likely not kill
> them, I would put it side-by-side in the utmost
> undesirable category.
>
> My ex-spouse and I were raised very differently
> and in different parts of the country, and often
> what he thinks is safe based on his experience of
> living in a rural county is different from what I
> think is safe. We also live in two geographic
> areas that vary in their crime levels. For me, I
> default to, "Would a judge agree with me?"

Beware of thinking, "Would my friends agree with me?" This is not a good rule of thumb because usually we hang out with people who have similar values. In the same way, the other parent's friends would probably agree with them. Maybe these guiding principles work for you or maybe you have different ones. Either way, I encourage you to think it through as it will help your co-parent to understand that your motives are not malicious.

Like a wedding anniversary, you will remember this day; it is significant. I encourage you to be mindful in bringing meaningful closure to what has been very difficult. While your grief process never really ends, my hope is that it's a lot less turbulent than when you first separated. You will encounter many suggestions along the way, but I truly believe only your internal compass will be able to determine what is right for you on this important day. *I encourage you to think it over and feel the emotions rather than pretend they're not there. It is important to your process.*

15

FORGIVING YOUR EX
BECAUSE YOU DESERVE IT

I KNOW THIS IS NOT THE CHAPTER YOU WANT TO READ. For many of us, it's upsetting simply to see the word "forgiving." My heart aches for you. Being surrounded by my faith community, I could hardly talk about anything without the rage of unforgiveness seeping into the conversation. It was grotesque, and I hated that when I was honest with myself, there was a part of me that wanted him to die. I wanted him to suffer; I thought he deserved it. As my hurting heart tried to make sense of why this was happening to me, I realized it was costing me quality of life to hold these feelings. I didn't want to be mad. I didn't want to stay stuck. Forgiveness is so much more satisfying than revenge. I knew I somehow had to figure out a way to not hate him, so I began what I call the pre-forgiveness stage.

Pre-forgiveness is opening your heart to the idea

that forgiveness may be an important part of your process. Yep, your process. I want to encourage you to take the next step in your healing journey towards forgiveness, not because the other person deserves it, not even because the Bible calls us to forgive, but because of the "why" behind forgiveness. There are very few things that I will claim with 100% certainty, but I'm going to stake my claim here: forgiving will benefit you tremendously. The hard work of authentically forgiving someone is life-changing.

Where to begin? Let's first look at the word "forgive." It is a verb, an action word. I want to encourage you to think of it as a process rather than a checkbox. Before we can even begin the forgiveness process, lets tap into a little Counseling Psychology 101: hurt people hurt people. Bear with me for a second. Can you consider the possibility that maybe your ex-spouse didn't do what they did with the specific intention of hurting you? That in all probability the pain they caused and quite likely are continuing to cause you, comes out of wounds they never healed from their childhood. Sometimes when we analyze the other contributing factors as to why things ended up the way they did, we can begin to view that person as a victim themself. While they might have done a whole host of wrong actions, what if they were statistically more prone to do them? In counseling we call this "psychoeducation": acquiring information on the relevant psychological topics. It can be very helpful in softening your heart.

You're going to hate this next part but I'm going to say it anyway — you're going to have to acknowledge each individual hurt that makes up your gaping wound from divorce. I'm not a fan of just lumping this whole giant mess into a ball and tossing it in the air. Healing will take some soul-searching. I would encourage you to write out each individual thing that they did to hurt you on a notecard. For example, if your ex-spouse had an affair, don't just write "cheated on me," break it out into all the things that go with that. For example, "spent family money on hotel rooms to be with someone else" or "missed many family dinners because he was with her instead of us." Warning: mark out a day for this with no kids around; it will be a gut-wrenching, sad day, but the relief you will find makes it so worth it.

The things you don't write down are going to be your triggers in the future. Just because you forget them now doesn't mean you can't forgive them as they arise. Triggers are nearly impossible to avoid but do the best you can. You can always revisit this activity as more information is revealed or new things come up.

For now, you've identified ALL the acts that have you stuck in anger and resentment: the ugly stuff. What now? I can only give suggestions; I don't have a perfect process because everyone's heart and hurts are so unique. I would recommend you do something with all those notecards you just wrote out. You may want to read them out one by one then toss them into the fireplace or rip the card in half. Maybe you want to speak them out then paint over the words or dip them in water to dissolve the ink. Maybe you're not ready to do anything yet — it's okay to be honest with yourself and just wait until the time feels right to release yourself from all the things. I do believe you'll reach a point when you're tired of hanging on to it all. It's okay to wait for that day.

This activity may sound simple, but I want to recognize in no way do I think it's easy. Forgiveness takes so much maturity and strength; it may be the most difficult part of your healing journey. I genuinely believe you can't move into a thriving state until you're able to truly sit in a state of forgiveness. When you're able to authentically give them the benefit of the doubt and consider they're not trying to be a jerk, even though it may have appeared that way all along. I just don't believe that it is anyone's intention, perhaps more accurately described as lack of intention, is to be a jerk. Their day to day unacceptable actions quite possibly are a result of their own childhood mechanics. The contributors of why your marriage ended were likely years in the making.

Furthermore, your best self doesn't want to continue the pain process of hurting more people out of the pain you have experienced. The cycle stops now. In case you didn't pick it up earlier in this book, I want to remind you: we teach people how to treat us. As we practice forgiveness, that doesn't mean "forgive and forget" (that's actually NOT in the Bible!); part of forgiveness is getting things different in relationships both past and present. I loved in Lysa TerKeurst's book *Forgiving What I Can't Forget* where she says, "Boundaries aren't to push others away, they're to protect ourselves." Sometimes part of forgiveness is analyzing what we could do different moving forward. What unacceptable behavior did you accept under the guise of love? You hear, "marriage is hard," but that doesn't mean you do nothing and don't talk about or problem-solve through the hard things.

Is part of what landed you in this Divorceland nightmare that you didn't talk about the hard things? Why not? Maybe it's the way it was in your family of origin? Or maybe you tried at first and it seemed to make things worse? In Alcoholics Anonymous there's a saying, "we're only as sick as our secrets." I know that my marriage got excessively worse and my ex-husband threatened divorce if I talked to anyone about what was going on in our marriage. This was probably one of the unhealthiest things I could have complied to. Now, I'm not saying tell anyone and everyone your deep marital struggles, but I am saying it's a huge red flag if you're not "allowed" to tell anyone. I encourage you to seek out and find those friends you can be fully transparent with — horrifyingly vulnerable. They are essential to your new self and future relationships. It's kind of like how they used to use canaries to sense toxic gas while mining because they were more sensitive to it. You need those friends moving forward who speak the hard truth in love because they care enough and vice versa. Please, please, please only listen to friends whose lives you respect.

After forgiveness comes redemption. I love that word: redemption. Based on the word "redeem," it's the idea that we are trading in something in exchange for something that we want more. When you forgive, you are trading the hostility that eats you up, for freedom and true joy. We all know that woman that stayed bitter and let divorce eat up any joy in her life; she never forgave, and she never recovered from divorce. I don't want this for you; I want you to find a way to understand the psychology of hurt and to release your hurts so they can just be scars from your past. You must view this as an active, ongoing process, and I will validate that it will be extremely hard, but so worth it. You can forgive, not because they deserve it, but because you do.

DATING ... AGAIN

FOR BEGINNERS

IF YOU'RE LIKE ME, the idea of dating again is horrifying. Like, it was bad enough the first time around, but the thought of doing it at this stage in life with kids is not appealing. However, the loneliness struggle is real, and dating is how you connect the dots. At the end of the day, this all has to be "worth it".

If you're not convinced it's worth it, or maybe you stick your toe in the pool and it makes you want to jump out of your skin ... well, maybe it's just not time yet. That is okay; give yourself time and listen to your heart. The reality is you've been through a lot. While many adhere to the one-year post-divorce finalization as a rough guideline, I say it's a minimum guideline. Don't beat yourself up if it just feels too soon. Having friends of the opposite sex may help you heal and work towards that goal, if that's your goal.

Maybe, like me, you enjoy doing life with someone.

Well, my hope is that you've found a same-sex friend to do life with in the meantime but … let's be real though, you want to have sex again, someday. Whatever your motivation is, I just want you to be aware of it. Just like when you try to lose weight, you need to know your "why" as a means to propel and guide you if you want to sustain the not fun part.

Step 1: Stabilize yourself. Hopefully, by the time you are considering dating, you have re-established who you are. You want to be sure that you have a strong sense of identity and what you want out of life. It's important that the waves of grief have stopped slamming you constantly — just maybe every once in a while. This is the Step 1 of the benchmarks that you are ready to date. If you have not done those, please don't proceed to Step 2. If you haven't yet found a stable sense of self and your own footing on the shore, you will get tossed around the dating ocean and be worse off.

Maybe you're so secure in your sense of self that you're afraid to enter the dating scene because it's not so bad alone; there are lots of perks. That's okay, too. Some people stay here because they truly are that happy by themselves … but don't stay there because you're scared. Sometimes we can do all our work but our final stages of healing and getting it different come out of changed life application.

You can't fix what you don't know is broken. You can't heal your trust issues if you hold everyone at arm's-length. My default survival tool is to not let anyone help me. If I have to depend on anyone then they will eventually leave or disappoint me, so I don't let them help me. This is not healthy and it's exhausting. I also miss going deeper in relationships because it's too scary to let them in. It's like never going to the ocean because I'm afraid I'll get eaten by a shark. Now, there's a million things that might cause me some pain if I go to the ocean, but all those things are worth it because I absolutely love the ocean.

For me, it's always the tension of "worth it." Let *worth it* be your guiding principle in dating. Continually ask yourself, "Are the things I'm doing *worth it* in the big picture of finding my next spouse?" If it's sucking up more time than you have to give, or coming at the cost of your relationship with your kids — re-evaluate if now is the time or if you can allot certain chunks of time so that it doesn't consume you.

Throughout this whole process I want you to envision yourself walking down a beautiful path in a setting that makes you happy. *Note: I didn't say walking toward the altar of marriage, that may be too overwhelming of an image at this point.* So that path is straight, your eyes are focused forward on where you're going. Now think of dating as people that come alongside you as you're walking and walk with you. You must authentically, 100% be "you" and that person walking alongside you had better be cheering for you, holding your hand, and doing nothing but supporting the lovely person that you have grown into. They should not be shifting or tampering or nudging you onto a different path. If so, let go of their hand on your walk and keep walking straight on your path until the next person comes along.

Let me propose the obvious yet horrifying question: where do you meet people?! You have to figure out what's right for you. Some people like bars, but it wasn't my scene. What I realized about the bar scene was that I'm never going to attract the guy I want based on my appearance. That my best assets are internal and I need/want him to like who I am on the inside ... and that just doesn't happen at bars ... but lots of other things do. Now I totally recognize they can be fun. I went through a phase where I had a lot of laughs trying to learn how to line dance, met some nice guys, but in the end, I recognized that it just wasn't my scene.

Also, I quickly realized that trying to get all your married friends to set you up with the one nice, single guy they know is not the best idea. He may be nice, but it doesn't mean he's a good match for you. And now you just made kid birthday parties awkward when you're both there. Better to meet at the birthday party and become friends. Those friends can be great for dipping your toe into the dating pool, even if it's just to commiserate on the struggle, and then maybe you can set each other up with other single friends.

One of the more curious things about making single opposite-sex friends later in life is that all of a sudden things can get misinterpreted or complicated in a way they didn't when you were married. When you went out with a co-worker of the opposite-sex for lunch when you were married, it wasn't weird ... now all of a sudden they might be thinking you're interested. I have no tips here, but just wanted to put it on your radar. But also, don't over assume that they're interested. In fact, just assume they're not unless they tell you otherwise. If it feels weird, ask another person to join you, and that should clarify how you view the lunch.

Try not to freak out every time someone of the opposite sex asks you to do something just you and them. Just chill out and enjoy the undefined time with them. You don't have to decide or define. I know I can say this and make it sound simple, but it's hard though, and I can make situations awkward quickly by trying to figure things out ... that really don't need to be defined.

Maybe a good way to widen your social circle is to get involved in a new activity you've always wanted to try, or join a club for something you already like doing. Whether it's a writing club or a volleyball team, it doesn't matter. You're just looking for someone who has similar interests. Now that you actually know who you are and how you like to spend your time, I strongly suggest you find someone like you. You will have so much more fun when you're not constantly compromising. I'm not saying get stuck in a rut doing the same old things; I'm saying if you're a foodie, go on a food tour, meet someone who also likes exploring adventurous new food options and alternate taking each other to your favorite spots or taking turns finding new ones to try together. When the focus is on the shared interest rather than on each other, it will be so much more comfortable.

I'm going to say the unthinkable ... try online dating! What? Yes, I know someone has mentioned it to you and there's such a stigma around it for *our generation,* but I think it's starting to lessen. I bet you'd be shocked how many of your friends met their spouse online if they were dating after 2005. I know I was! I feel like so many of my friends told me individually that they met their spouse online initially and I had no idea! One of the reasons I really like the idea of it is because of the sheer numbers game. That when I looked at the circles I ran and the number of single men I bumped into, there were slim pickings! I needed a bigger pond.

Step 2: Figure out what you're looking for. Take the reins, figure out what your deal breaker things are ... pause ... let's write them here:

1. _____
2. _____
3. _____

Secondly, what qualities are really important to you? In fact, I'm going to give you a nice little list of ideas here. Check the boxes of the things that are important and maybe add a few in the blanks at the bottom.

- Makes as much/more money than me
- Has gone to counseling post-divorce
- Has a family I enjoy being around
- Has a good co-parenting relationship
- Has an established career
- Takes good care of their body
- Has at least 40% custody
- Enjoys their kids
- Likes to hike
- Likes to cook
- Keeps a clean house
- Likes to go to concerts
- Is happy
- Has a dog
- Doesn't have a dog
- Is a positive person
- Volunteers
- Likes to vacation
- Owns a house
- Plays an instrument
- Eats healthy
- Has good teeth
- Has great eyes

- Enjoys their job
- Is a morning person
- Is polite
- Has close same-sex friends
- Is vegan
- Is classy
- Is a good dresser
- Same religion as me
- Wants more kids
- Likes to take bike rides
- Dependable
- Ambitious
- Creative
- Likes to read
- Coffee drinker
- Appreciates good wine
- _____
- _____
- _____
- _____

After you checked your boxes, star your top three. This list will really help you after a first date. I want you to come back here and stay true to it. Swear to me that you won't try to alter your list to match the person you just went on a first date with. You have got to be true to your needs and wants if you want to get it different this time. You didn't come this far to do the same dang thing! Realistically you won't know all the answers after your first date, but you can keep revisiting your list as more is revealed, and more than anything, I want you to pay attention to the things you are *not* okay with and stay firm on those.

One of things that stood out to me was if they had little or no official custody schedule. To me, this signified that they don't value those relationships. I wanted to be with a man who values the relationships with his kids so that if things worked out, he would value my kids, too ... and not make me pick between him or my kids — he would just get it. It doesn't matter what your list looks like, I just want this to be about you having enough self-worth to value what you want.

There is a TED Talk by Christina Wallace where she introduced the idea of the Zero Date. I have a link on my website *(Surviving2Thriving.life)* if you want to give it a quick listen — it's five minutes long, funny and relevant. I must say, this TED Talk revolutionized the way I online dated. Prior to this, I waited for Mr. Right to reach out to me. I was not impressed; they were never what I was looking for, but I grew up thinking that it was a lady's role to be pursued. Here's the reality: I don't wait for things to happen to me in any other area of life, so why would I in this area? In the end, I needed a guy that was okay with my moxie and if he couldn't handle me starting the conversation, then he probably wasn't a good fit anyway.

Honestly, I was hesitant to write this chapter because dating is so different for everyone. I just want you to think through it and find the *intentional* style of dating for you. I can have a lot of opinions, but honestly, I can be easily convinced that there is more than one right way. Here is my rendition of what Christina Wallace suggested:

1. Make the obnoxious dating profile. Don't let a friend do it because you want it to accurately reflect "you" and the way you talk/are. You can cheat and read blogs about how to do this if you want.
2. Make your lists above to specify what your criteria is.
3. Don't wait for Mr. Wrong to reach out to you, proactively seek out Mr. Right.
4. Ask them on a very short "Zero Date."
5. Reflect on your "Zero Date."
6. Gently let them know how you want to proceed.
7. Repeat Steps 1-6 until you find someone you want to have an official first date with.

In more detail …

Step 3: Reaching out to Mr. Right. Figure out how much time you are willing to spend on this. Don't let it suck up your life or unintentionally take away from your time with your kids. Also go for quality messages over quantity. Try to comment on something specific in their profile that you have in common and then ask them a question that provokes a conversation. For example, "I saw on your profile you like to read. I'm reading Jodi Piccoult's book *The Book of Two Ways*. What are you reading?" Casual and simple. Try setting a goal like sending one message a day or whatever feels like the right amount to you. Maybe it's time blocking like twenty minutes, three times a week. There's no right answer, so figure out what works for you.

Steps 4: The Art of the "Zero Date." Have a small amount of conversation back and forth, then ask them on a very short "Zero Date" that is relevant to some of the conversation you've had about your shared interests. It should be an hour or less. Coffee or a drink, a beach walk (though that can be kinda limiting on what you can wear), or maybe it's even a group activity, like a church event. This is your rip-the-band-aid-off moment. Stop wasting your time talking on the phone and texting back and forth with someone you have no chemistry with. For example, one of the things I had to figure out was, am I attracted to bald guys? I know, that sounds so insensitive. But I also knew that one of my criteria was being with a guy I couldn't keep my hands off. I didn't have it in my first marriage, but I knew it was possible from previous dating experiences. And guess what? You don't know if you're going to want to kiss someone unless you're in proximity to them. Regardless, chemistry is absolutely a real thing and, in my personal and professional opinion, ideal in marriage. Can marriages survive without it? Yep, all the time, but since we're making a wish list, why not try?

I also love the "Zero Date" because of your ability to easily end a bad date. Oh man, sometimes no matter how good a person looks on paper, it's a really terrible date in person. Before I knew about this wonderful concept, I went on one date so bad that I considered "going to the bathroom" and just leaving him at the table. If you know me (which I recognize you don't), you know that's totally not my style. And here's the truth, the date went so horribly awry that I wish I listened to my gut and left! Boy, did I wish I had that hard stop essential to the "Zero Date." And hey, if you want to be pursued, there's plenty of opportunity for that with the second date. Maybe that's part of your criteria, "Must ask me on a second date within 48 hours."

Steps 5 & 6: Taking time to reflect is critical! Get in your car or go in your room, turn the radio off and think. Get your list out and think of it in context of the person you just met. There were several times the moment I walked away from the "Zero Date" that I thought that person might be a fit, and even agreed to plans for a second date. Then later I'd think about my list and realize that person was missing the mark for what I was looking for. Just because you agreed to a second date doesn't mean you have to go on it. I do encourage kindness though. Maybe breaking the plans will look something like this, "Hey, I had fun getting to know you today and you seem like a fun person but after thinking about it a little more, I don't think you're a good fit for me. Thanks for the coffee and best of luck on your dating journey!" In my experience, the person on the receiving end was actually really cool about it and replied that they appreciated me not wasting their time or something along those lines. If they try to convince you to go on a second date, block their number. I know that might sound harsh but I think it's necessary in order to listen to your gut and stay strong.

Step 7: Find your pace. Something I've come to recognize about myself is that I'm extremely loyal. So as far as dating, I can only do this process one guy at a time. I realized early on I cannot "casually" date multiple people. I understand that's me and not everyone. I point it out because that's what worked for me, and lots of people do otherwise. I just realized that it was important for me to stay true to that. I felt dating multiple people added a level of stress and complication that wasn't worth it to me. I was fairly happy by myself and not in a huge rush to remarry. To each their own.

Whatever you do, wait to sleep with them. Wait until you know you want to spend your life with them, because once you start having sex, you won't be able to see clearly and it's very hard to walk away if you see red flags. For some people, there is a religious element here. I can't tell you exactly where this timeline falls, but I can tell you that casual sex in the early dating stage will definitely have you blundering through some pain. Do it for yourself because you deserve more. You've come this far and put in so much effort trying to get it right, so don't let your hormones guide you. It's not about self-control (okay maybe a little), but when you're focused on what you want and who you want to be, it will be a whole lot easier to hold on to your gumption.

Also, there's definitely something to setting yourself up for success. If you found Mr. McDreamy and you guys have awesome chemistry, that is truly wonderful … but if you think you're going to go watch a movie in a house with just the two of you at night and keep your hands to yourself … you're wrong. Also, let me remind you that alcohol lowers your inhibitions. You know those things you feel strongly about? Well, they may not seem so important after a few drinks. Just saying — think it through and be intentional just like you have with so many other things along the way.

You found someone you want to date exclusively, and you think they're pretty awesome, good for you! You remember that visual I gave you at the start of the beginning of this chapter of walking down a path and allowing other people to walk alongside you? Are you still walking your path? What does it look like visually in that analogy to see that person? Do you like how your life has changed since they have come onto the scene? There are two types of post-divorcees: those that have done their work, and those that have not. Pleeeeeease tell me you have chosen someone that has. Slow things down if not.

You realize you are in the best part now? Okay in some ways, there's definitely an argument for like when you're in your sixties if your marriage is going strong, kids out of the house, established career, maybe some traveling ... sounds pretty sweet living the dream. So maybe a close second is now. When you have all the blissful happy feelings about this wonderful person that is enhancing your life experience, enjoy it. Take it in.

Family blending is hard. While it's important for your kids to meet this person, it's really hard on them if you break up, especially if you do that several times. Get yourselves right first. Have conversations about what the ideal introduction timeline might be and how it would look. While you want to be mindful of when to introduce the kids, don't be afraid to tell them about the person. Let their curiosity build.

Let them know all the reasons you like that person and what kind of things you guys do together. Tell them funny stories about that person or silly things that happened. Let them know that you don't want them to meet them yet because you know that if they meet him, they're going to like him so much that you might keep him around just because how awesome he is with them. And you need things to be awesome as a couple because you don't want to go through another divorce. FYI – breakups and divorce are the same thing for kids ten and under.

All the buildup will get them excited. Talking about your special someone will give them a lens to frame that person positively within, and increase the likelihood of things going well. This is super important because if your kids don't love him, it's going to be a compounding effect. It's already hard to raise someone else's kids, and it's very unlikely they are going to love them the way you do. How your kids come to meet this individual is going to set the tone for their relationship to come so put some effort into getting it off to a strong start.

If necessary, due to various custody situations they see your special someone that's okay, waving is okay, even brief conversation. You just want to avoid any kind of attachment or hanging out at your house when your kids are there. No gifts yet either.

What about spending the night once he or she has met the kids? Well, that entirely depends on what you are trying to teach your children in this area. If you are okay with them sleeping around (because your sixteen-year-old daughter will absolutely throw it in your face as equivalent), then go for it. But if you want to model something else, then set the standard yourself. I'm not here to judge or tell you what's right or wrong, I just want you to be aware of the implications for you to make a conscious decision.

As your dating relationship progresses, I want you to continually self-assess whether you are able and encouraged to be fully "you" while in relationship with this person.

Honestly, the biggest adjustment for me was the time suck. Okay, totally worth it because I love my second husband to pieces and genuinely enjoy being with him, like really a lot, but he was crashing my productivity. I decided that my quality of life was better with him in it, though. Those feelings of loneliness suck! … Like how long would it take someone to find my dead body if I keeled over right now? No? Is it just me who has morbid thoughts like that? I know I'm not alone!

While you have your list and that person checks your most important boxes, the reality is that no one is perfect and second marriages are hard. The phrase that I started telling my now husband over and over again was "this is worth it." Any family blending situation is going to be difficult, even if only one of you has children. There are varying degrees in that struggle, but the question I would encourage you to really process through is: "Is all the good he brings to the table worth the hard stuff?" I'm certain that your gut response is, "yeah, sure" but I really want you to think through it and have some intentional conversations with your kids. Be sure to ask them open-ended questions on the subject; the more they can feel onboard with the decision, the more likely you can point them back to the big vision of being "worth it" when things get hard.

There is a simplicity that comes with being single. Are you ready to give that up? Again, I really want you to not get caught up in the romance and lose your logical brain to holistically analyze the situation. I just want you to go into a second marriage with eyes wide open, fully informed. If you don't know the flaws of your significant other, do not get engaged until you have figured that out.

I don't know what you're looking for in a life partner but it's essential that you know and that the next person you marry is all the really important things to you. I want to be clear, my expectation of Husband #2 was never perfection. It's just someone who cares enough to have the hard conversations when my heart is hurt and to problem-solve solutions. I just want a guy that's as crazy about me as I am him. I wanted someone who not only likes but truly appreciates me just as I am, that wasn't going to try to change or mold me. Someone I could look at our life with and sometimes just laugh at the sheer chaos of signing up to raise six kids together! When we got married, our kids were every single age between 7-14 except 11 years old! It's often hard but I'm really happy with my choice where the good things outweigh all the hard stuff.

This life honestly looks quite different than the one I imagined but I love it … most of the time. We have a crappy custody schedule that forces us to be in two different states way more than I'd like. Good thing I love my independence! When I look at my experience in youth ministry and school counseling, I think I was perfectly designed to be the mom of a large family. There are so many things that just feel like a perfect fit. There are also things that are really hard, but those things don't have anything on the good things.

Now that you know who you are and where you're heading, honestly ask yourself if this person is going to grow you into more of that, or is this person going to crush your spirit and all the hard work you've done? I hope and pray that it's the first — That any negatives are hands-down worth it. If you're not sure, wait! Time will tell. Whatever path you choose will have its challenges; my prayer is that the path you pick brings you closer to your purpose.

CLOSING THOUGHTS &
ACKNOWLEDGEMENTS

I hope this book has inspired you to be your best self. I'd love to hear from you, your story and what you want me to write more of as I continue my journey. You can find me on my website: *Surviving2Thriving.life*. There are lots of great, free resources to help you rebuild yourself and support you as you reestablish your adjusted family. I definitely don't have all the answers, but I have lots of ideas! My heart is for healing families.

I am so grateful for my own family who lovingly supported and continues to support my own crazy journey of life. They were great listeners and so patient. To my sister, Ashley Minnich, and her family who welcomed me into their home for long weekends and helped me catch my breath. For showing up, for making me a priority, and loving on me even though I'm sure I was a handful. To my parents, Ben and

Michelle Day, who stood by what I'm sure was very hard to watch and offered support any way they could think of; for being patient and kind even when I wasn't. Dad, thanks for gently saying the hard things. Mom, for always trying, caring and sacrificing.

I would have never started this journey to true living if it weren't for Marianne Allen, the pastoral counselor who I first saw with my ex-husband. She got me to stop accepting unacceptable behavior, spoke pure truth that struck my heart and changed my life. She guided me through my worst days of surviving and pushed me forward, as I began to believe that I could not only recover from divorce but actually be better off. For being patient with me as I argued like an attorney, questioning most everything she said, only to realize again and again that she was right. For believing in me more than I ever believed in myself and gently planting seeds for years to write this book! Also, for convincing me to stay in it with Steve when I wanted to give up — he might be my best decision yet.

I'm grateful for my incredible women's bible study group at Saddleback Church's Corona Campus who held me up early on when I felt like I couldn't take one more step. Specifically, Cari Burnett and Belinda Williamson who loved me in the most godly way. Saddleback Church recalibrated my understanding of what it means to love and extend grace in a beautiful way I didn't even know was possible. Their actions deepened my understanding of how we are called to love like Jesus.

To Jaime for being "my person" in the early days, saying the unthinkable things I didn't want to admit to, and for teaching me to play the "At Least" game and a lot of laughs when it seemed impossible. For the many amazing friends who brought meals, helped with childcare and just sat in my yucky emotions with me. To Ronald Tran, a dear childhood friend, who stepped in at just the right time to encourage me to stay on the path I am called to, even when the world was telling me otherwise — you made a huge difference. To my bestie for life, Adair Hawkins, I don't even know where to start. I suppose I should start with thanking you for the many phone calls as I verbally processed the unthinkable reality that I was living in, and for your encouraging words. Katie, for cheering me up time and time again. To all Harvest Christian School mommy friends who helped with logistics and didn't ask why I was wearing sunglasses inside. To Principal/Pastor Forrest for helping me believe that my kids will be okay. To Carol Plowman for the many dinners out when it all just felt like too much.

To my boss, Marla Maynard, thanks for not firing when my life blew up in my face. For letting me walk away from the counseling profession when I needed to, and for being my biggest cheerleader and welcoming me back into it with open arms when the time was right. Your wisdom, love, and encouragement have deeply impacted my path. I will always be grateful.

To my incredible current husband and best friend, Steve Commisso, who loves me in a way I was completely unfamiliar with. I love our story and from tipsy tennis to nerding out together. He has rocked my world and expectations on every level — in a way I didn't even know was possible. May our scars always keep us appreciating the love that we share. I love doing life with him and our crazy circus of six kids a.k.a. "The Pack." I wake up every day still somewhat surprised and delighted that he's my person.

My bio kids are kind of rockstars. Pastor Forrest was right; while it may seem like they will die if I don't feed them every two hours, they are actually tremendously resilient kiddos. I have stretched them and they have risen to the occasion. We have learned so much on this crazy journey of life together. I truly believe they are better because of the hard stuff. They have built skills and knowledge that will serve them well for life. It is truly a pleasure to be their mama!

While my bonus kids came as quite the surprise, they have already taught me so much. I appreciate their patience with me as I stretch into this new, unchartered territory of "bonus mom." I am every day deeply grateful how they have accepted me with open arms. I look forward to building many fun memories in the future.

I'm thankful for all of my content readers, many

already mentioned above but also: Justin i.
helping find my voice, and Pam Ollar. .
contributed to shaping this book and encouraged m
move forward. Thank you.

Last and certainly not least, to my editor, Samantha Jaquez. For making my words more readable, painstakingly pushing my voice through, making sense of my jumbled thoughts, and trying to apply grammar that makes sense. I appreciate your patience as my crazy life unfolded to make this book a reality. It was truly a pleasure working with you!

ABOUT THE AUTHOR

Torrey is a Licensed Professional Clinical Counselor (LPCC) with a thriving private practice in Orange County, California. She earned her bachelors in Psychology from Seattle Pacific University and a masters in Educational Counseling later respecializing in Clinical Counseling from Azusa Pacific University. Torrey is a mother, wife, therapist, author and speaker. After suffering her own post-divorce fallout in 2016, Torrey has transformed her pain into purpose and has a passion to support divorced, single parents to do the same.

TherapywithTorrey.com

instagram.com/TorreytheTherapist